It Was God

The Natalie Nichole Story

A true story, based on events in the life of Natalie Nichole, in her own words.

Natalie Nichole Enterprise
#1022
11700 Preston Rd. STE 720
Dallas Texas, 75230
Phone: 917-719-5637

Social Media:
www.NatalieNichole.com
ShopNatalieNichole.com
IG: @Natalie_Moments

© 2021 Natalie Nichole | Natalie Nichole Enterprise

CONTENTS

A Message From Natalie Nichole 1

1. You Are My Sunshine 3
2. The Early Years 5
3. Mister Tremaine 16
4. Always Be My Baby 24
5. Mastering Overcoming Boundaries 31
6. The Great Escape 51
7. Homeless For The Calling 57
8. Overdue 62
9. Becoming The Queen Dove 83

Reflections 90

A Message From Natalie Nichole

I didn't want to write a typical biography because I'm still young, and my life story will be ongoing well after this book is released. With that said, I wanted to put out a book about my life up to this point as a foundation for people to know the essence of Natalie Nichole, be able to relate, and continue to watch me build and rise from here. I attempted writing my book in 2012, but didn't quite like the direction it was going because it felt cliche.

This time, I took a different approach, thanks to Carl Michel's Write A Legacy workshop. Instead of speaking on my life as if I didn't live it and as if you are reading some God did it all type book, I wanted to throw you into my life as if you were there with me.

I'm a young Christian woman who knows where her water comes from, but by no means am I perfect. So yes, you're about to read a book that's realistic, full of sarcasm, possibly some swear words, spirituality, faith, and sin. I'm basically writing a book about a human that doesn't sugar-coat anything, and who values each life lesson encountered. I'm an honest individual, and I don't hide my flaws or missteps. I always call out my imperfections, so I can continue to evolve. With me, what you see is what you get. Whether you like me or agree with my perspective, is none of my business. I just wanted this book out for my future descendants and anyone else that might appreciate the beauty and testimony of my story.

I never considered myself an author until now, but I definitely have always been a writer. If you know me personally or are a fan of mine, you know exactly what I mean when I say that. If you aren't familiar with me and this is your intro to Natalie Nichole, you'll put two and two together by the end of this read. Please enjoy. I hope you take something away from my story and that it inspires you in more ways than one.

1
You Are My Sunshine

In the beginning, there was a lit-tle Gura..

I was born September 17th, 1994 in Lubbock, Texas. My only memories of Lubbock were my sister's father coming home from work while it was snowing. He had chicken fried steak, picked me up by my toes, and swung me around in a circle before putting me on his shoulders to walk in to the house. That was one of the more fond memories.

Another memory was of Mr. Anderson across the street, always giving me peanut butter bars and watching the comings and goings of my mom, sister, and I. Mr. Anderson was a sweet old man that loved how we always looked like we were on a mission.

A darker memory I recall, while briefly living in Lubbock, was being molested. To be honest, though, it's very vague in my mind. I can picture it happening. I can see who it was, but like I said, it's a brief memory.

My mom, sister, and I moved to San Antonio, Texas when I was four years old, so you can understand why my memory of Lubbock is murky.

Knowing my life story/testimony to date, I can't say my short-lived experiences in Lubbock were even a fraction of what I was to experience during the rest of my upbringing. You're probably wondering why I named this chapter "You Are My Sunshine" starting with very little, but to me there's a lot more sunshine contained in this chapter than what you're about to read. Another reason is because my mom sang that song to me all the time as a kid, and we'd remix the words together. I even had a little lion where you could pull his tail and it would play that tune. I still have that lion to this day. Sunshine was my hope, and luckily I had a few rays to carry with me throughout my life.

With all that said, let's really dive in!

2
The Early Years

Molestation | She said goodbye | Daddy's Home

I dealt with molestation at a very young age. One of the first memories I have of an occurrence, I had to be no older than three years old. I was living in Lubbock, and the individuals that took advantage of me were two cousins of mine. One cousin was from my sister's father's side of the family. The other perpetrator was from my mother's side of the family.

All I can really remember from those moments, was being touched in inappropriate places, and it being when no one else was around. Thankfully, those experiences were short-lived and not repeated. Unfortunately, I wasn't able to leave these types of occurrences behind in Lubbock. It eventually happened again.

When we moved from Lubbock to San Antonio, it was the year of "The Flood of 1998." Upon arrival, we moved in with one of my favorite aunts, but our stay didn't last long.

The dynamic of my mother's side of the family is very difficult to explain. They often choose not to speak to one another for years to decades for no apparent reason. But that's a book I'll have to leave for my mother to write about. I assume that type of behavior stems from their own childhood traumas and upbringing.

We ended up renting a home from my aunt that was two blocks away from her, in a subdivision that we really couldn't afford. We lived in that neighborhood for about nine months before finding another place in a run down cul-de-sac on a street called Palm Park Blvd. At the time, run down was all that we could afford, with only one parent fitting the bill.

I would've liked to think anything with the word *palm* in it would represent something pleasant, beautiful, or even tropical, but that wasn't the case. This house was falling apart and infested with every type of insect you could imagine. It was an awkward green and white color with bright green matted carpet to match it on the inside. Sometimes maggots would come up from the carpet. That's how disgusting this house was. My mother is a clean, organized person, so for us to live in a place like that, you can just imagine the horror we all experienced.

We lived on Palm Park Blvd for about two years. I can't say I have any terrible memories there, if you don't take into account the snakes crawling through the living room window, scorpions popping up in random places like the showerhead, and that awful, bright green matted carpet.

We lived in the country and had lots of cats. They helped with some of the insect and rodent problems, but it didn't quite help with the flea infestation. It was so bad, the exterminator swiped a white rag on the grass, and it came back black.

My mom worked from home, and I took the bus to and from school. I remember being this quirky, but headstrong, six year old kid walking home and whistling random tunes. I have an abnormally high-pitched whistle, and my mother could always hear me from a block away at the bus stop. Everyone knew when Lit-tle Gura was coming home.

Between 2000-2003, so much happened in my life, that it all runs together for me. My sense of time was based more off of events rather than actual dates and times. This part of my story is difficult to tell in it's entirety, but my mother could tell it better. My grandmother was diagnosed with cancer, and passed away shortly after, on May 4th, 2001. I've often had dreams of her, as if she were there to give approval of how I've navigated my journey.

An impactful moment involving my grandmother, happened the weekend she passed away. I find this event imperative to tell because it shines a light on my intuitive senses with things others can't always see. Each weekend before her passing, Mother drove us all to visit her in Lubbock.

My grandmother only spoke Spanish. It was frustrating, because how was I supposed to have conversations with her if I didn't speak the same language? I wish that I would've had the opportunity to know her better and that language wasn't a barrier between us. My innovative mom made my big sister and I listen to the Tejano station to learn Spanish. We reluctantly ended up learning every Spanish song that existed at the time. My mom's original plan only required us to learn two songs in the hopes that we'd pick up some words or phrases with each listen. Ultimately, we did. But my goodness! We definitely got more than we bargained for.

The night before my grandmother's passing, I dreamt her. I remember rolling over, looking to the side of the bed in the middle of the night to see a blue mist of someone that resembled an older version of my mother. I rolled back over, unfazed, and immediately fell back to sleep.

The next morning while we were getting dressed for our trip to Lubbock, an interesting series of events occurred. Nothing seemed out of the ordinary, until my mother heard her name being called. However, no one else was in the house but the two of us. Her phone then began to ring. Naturally, we both went into the living room to find and answer the phone, only to discover that her cell phone was completely turned off.

Moments later, we both heard the front screen door slam harder than usual, making us both react with a jolt. We had a lot of cats around, so we were used to them playing with the door. When we opened the door, expecting to see our pets playing on the front porch, there was absolutely nothing in sight.

I asked my mother what was going on, a little freaked out about the situation, and she couldn't muster up an answer. We continued getting ready for the drive. On this particular trip, we were driving with my mom's older sister and my cousin.

We weren't too far outside of San Antonio, before we received a call from my uncle asking us to pull over. He then delivered the news that my grandmother had passed on. He also told us the time of my grandmother's death. One of my mother's sisters, that was present while my grandmother passed, mentioned she was breathing heavily right before she died.

The time of her death happened to be around the same time we experienced my mother hearing her name being called, the phone ringing even though it was off, and the screen door slamming with no wind or anyone outside to cause it. I took note of everything. Later on, my mother told me that her mother always wondered if people said goodbye to their loved ones when they were about to pass. I guess she answered her own question.

Sometime in 2002, we moved to a beautiful house on five acres of land in a nice subdivision called Tierra Mesa in the city of China Grove. Since my aunt and cousin had just moved into town, we tended to be at their house often. I feel like my older cousin took advantage of that. He molested me from when I was six to ten years old. I remember him being inappropriate with me while we were left alone or when he'd babysit me. I felt inferior when his friends were around, as if they knew exactly what he was doing to me on the low. I was embarrassed to be around them, and felt like an outcast.

When you're being groomed to tolerate inappropriate things, you're often confused on knowing the difference between what's right and wrong. You get manipulated into believing everything your perpetrator does is justified because they're older, have the power, and there's nothing you can do about it. At the age of seven, you are yet to even develop a need to protect yourself. While enduring this male figure's presence in my life, I yearned for someone to protect me.

Around the time I turned eight, I inquired to my mother about my biological father. My mother never hid knowledge about my father from me, but up to that point, I had never even seen a picture of him. I was told he was out there somewhere and that he was black, which made me half black. At that age, I didn't even understand what being mixed really meant. I knew that I was still loved in spite of that.

I kept pressing my mother about meeting my father, because I wanted to know that part of myself. I thought meeting him would make some huge difference in my life, and I'd have a sense of security or wholeness like I'd seen happen in the movies. My mother then took the initiative. She made it happen with the help of her then boss, Mr. McGee, who I consider a surrogate grandfather. We did some research and found out that my father lived in Lubbock at the time. When we got in contact with him, he requested to meet us in Abilene at his mother's ranch. I remember talking on the phone with both my grandmother and father before we planned our trip to officially meet. My grandmother couldn't hold her composure, as she was so excited to finally chat. My father tried to play it cool with his smooth, low voice.

After speaking with my father and grandmother, my mother got me on the phone with my daddy, my sister's father, who still lived in Lubbock. He wasn't fond of the fact that I was going to meet my biological father. I remember Daddy crying on the phone saying he loved me and that I would always be his daughter. In trying to comfort the man that gave me his last name and treated me like his own, I told him with certainty and tenderness "It's okay, Daddy. I still love you. You're still my Daddy, and nothing will ever change that."

To this day, I appreciate him so much for the little things he did for me when I was around him. He'd take me to the park down the street from Grandma's house, let me adopt tumbleweeds, and then we'd hunt for horntoads. He's the only man I'll ever call Daddy. I'll always have a special place in my heart for him, choosing to love me when he didn't have to.

It was a brief and impactful event going to meet my biological father. We only spent three days together. The days leading up to meeting him, I was excited like any young girl meeting her father for the first time would be. I definitely romanticized the whole situation.

My mom and I drove to Abilene. I remember it being dark when we arrived. We met my father at a grocery store parking lot, then headed to my grandmother's ranch. As we pulled into a parking space, ironically the song "Daddy's Home" by Shep and the Limelites began to play on the radio. This moment felt magical, like it was meant to be. It was something I never knew I needed.

My mother and I got out of the truck, and that's when I saw my father standing next to my uncles. I was taken aback, and couldn't muster up any words other than, "You drive a blue Mustang! That's my favorite type of car!" Shortly after my excited outburst, we exchanged pleasantries.

I asked my mom if I could ride to the ranch with my father. Thankfully, she agreed, pleased to witness my happiness. I jumped into the passenger seat of my dad's car, smiling from ear to ear. My father turned up the radio and punk rock music played in the background. I remember thinking wow, my dad likes this kind of music too?! Everything felt absolutely perfect. It was late by the time we pulled into the ranch. Mommy and I were shown to our room. I could hardly wait until morning.

After breakfast with my grandmother, I rode my bike around the ranch. I also got to feed a bull and play with stray kittens. Before the trip was over, my father promised he'd be there for me from that moment on. For someone who hadn't yet experienced disillusionment, I believed him wholeheartedly.

Months passed. My mom told me that he requested a paternity test. We went to court, did the test, and it was proved with 99.9% accuracy that I was his child. The court ordered my father to pay child support and asked him if he wanted to legally change my last name from Carrizalez to Williams. He let me keep my name. At most, my father ended up only paying two months of child support. One of the last things he sent me was a letter with a portion of a contradictory poem similar to "Two Dead Boys" by Tyler Rager.

My father comes across as intelligent, intuitive, and emotional. He tends to express himself through facts, literary pieces, quotes, and dark analogies. To me, his way of communicating through the poem, depicted him as someone who is neither here nor there. I feel as though our thought processes are similar, but our reactions to those thoughts, differ.

I was now plagued with confusion by meeting my father and him not truly stepping up to the plate. His neglect began to settle in. I now felt undervalued. This feeling transcended into my relationships with other males, including the grooming I was experiencing involving my cousin, who now lived with my family and I. I was disoriented, thinking that what he was doing to me was love.

I remember him nonchalantly revealing himself to me at times and making me touch near his genitals while he'd touch mine. There were times he'd lie beside me aroused and would press himself against me. I didn't fully understand what was happening. These events occurred often, until my mom made my aunt and cousin move out due to a new man in her life.

One starry night after my aunt and cousin had moved out, my mother and I were sitting on the front porch listening to oldies like we often did. Mommy always liked to share her life stories, wisdom, and jokes. I enjoyed listening to all her stories over and over again. Each time she spoke about her life, I could visualize everything. My mother could remember every detail of the major points and lessons of her life as if they'd just happened. Listening to her speak was like listening to a teacher run through the most intriguing lesson plan you'd ever heard. Each time she shared, I learned something new from it.

It's a lot like reading the Word. Every time you read the Bible, you learn something new depending on what stage of life you are in. I like to think I got my storytelling abilities from my mother. I've never asked her, but I'd hope she'd think the same.

She was always open with me, so it wasn't unusual for us to bring up touchy topics. "See the Funny Little Clown" by Bobby Goldsboro began to play while she brought up traumatic experiences she had when she was around my age. My mom turned up the radio and began to explain the words in the song, as if I didn't already know exactly what Bobby meant. Every day that I remained silent, a little more of my innocence died, but all everyone saw was a happy child.

After four years of enduring the abuse and overwhelmed with emotion, I ran into the house and began pacing back and forth. I was ready to tell my mother about what happened to me. The only thing I could think to do was to grab a doll from my room and bring it outside with me. My mother's intuition must've kicked in, because she asked me if anything inappropriate had ever happened to me.

I had yearned to tell her for so long, but at the same time I was nervous to break the news. Never good at lying, I timidly nodded. My mother was shocked and asked me for details about who it was. I demonstrated what happened to me with the doll. We both cried as I finally summoned up the courage to say who it was.

My mother immediately called my aunt, said we were on our way, and that she needed to speak with my cousin upon arrival. When my mother is in defense mode, you don't want to cross paths with her, she'll make you sorry you ever did. Driving to my cousin's house was the longest ride I'd ever taken in my life. I was sitting in the backseat, dreading our arrival. I purposely pretended to be asleep so I wouldn't have to face my abuser while my mother confronted him. I'm the type of person that avoids confrontation at all costs. I don't like feeling like I'm the cause of other people's problems.

We arrived to my aunt's apartment and waited for my cousin to come outside. My mother made him get in the passenger seat. I was still pretending to be asleep in the back. I listened in on their entire conversation, which was brief and direct. He surprisingly admitted to molesting me after my mother threatened him.

"Don't you ever think you can be alone or near my child again. I could report you, and they would throw you in jail. People in there would probably do the same things to your sorry ass."

I remember her saying she'd ask me if I wanted to report him, and if I said yes, she'd do it. The next day she asked me what I wanted to do. Somehow, even as a young girl, I knew that if I reported him, it could affect his future. I tend to look at situations from multiple perspectives, so when trying to make the best decision, I wasn't just considering how it impacted me. I knew I was going to have to find a way to heal and not be defeated. I decided not to turn him in. In my mind, not reporting him was my way of giving him a chance to change.

It's not in my heart to hurt others as some have done to me. As the saying goes, no matter how good you are, you are the bad guy in someone's story.

3

Mister Tremaine

Intro to Racism | Evil Step Dad

The first four years of my academic career, I was blessed to go to a multicultural district. Starting over was never an issue for me, because I never got too attached to anyone or anything. Despite the fact that I was used to being alone, experiencing so many changes in such a short time, left me feeling broken. I was trying to process my life up to that point. I felt lost and undeserving of happiness. I didn't even want to exist at times. I was becoming a pre-teen, and every new emotion I experienced was beginning to invade the little childhood I had left. The only things that made sense to me were dancing, songwriting, playing outside, and singing Mariah Carey songs at the top of my lungs.

Experiencing racism didn't really hit me until I was in fifth grade and moved to the southwest side of town. I always knew I was mixed and was proud to be both black and hispanic. I didn't realize that my race would eventually play a huge factor in how I was treated.

In school, the kids were oblivious to the hurtful things they'd say. A boy in my fifth grade class was the first person to ever call me the N-word. We were in the same group doing a class project. I don't know what made him think he could test me that day. He started randomly making fun of me and calling me a bitch and using the word fuck. I tried ignoring his remarks, but he persisted. I could usually handle simple name-calling, but my patience was wearing thin. I wasn't prepared to be insulted by anyone, let alone my fifth grade crush.

My teacher watched the entire verbal attack, and I wondered why he didn't intervene. After all the other mean things he said, the boy then called me the N-word. Up to that point, I was able to remain composed. But then that word flew out of his mouth. My blood boiled, as a fierce rage came upon me. I remember calmly stating, "Say it again." I repeated myself at least three times.

If he said it a third time, I'd strike. He did. With all my might, I slapped the shit out of him. Everyone in the classroom turned towards us, likely shocked at the sound of my palm as it struck his cheek. I left a red imprint of my hand on his face.

My teacher called me to his desk. With frustration overtaking me and tears streaming down my face, I'll never forget what he said. "Is there anything you want me to do, Natalie?" I looked at him, feeling disgusted.

I wanted to say, *Duh! You saw the entire thing happen and didn't stop it or protect me. Of course I want you to do something!* With a little pride and a whole lot of hurt, I instead responded with "No, I think I hit him hard enough."

After that, I became more aware of racism all around me. I had no idea people could be so hateful because of the color of my skin or by what they assumed about me. That incident wasn't the last time I encountered the burn of racism. There was a minefield of other racist events for me to navigate in the future.

My mother got married on March 24th, 2005. This was the beginning of a new era of suffering for me. From the moment I met this man, something was off about him. I saw the ugly in him. The evil seeped out of him like old, molding goo. We moved from the house I loved into my new stepfather's house. For the purposes of this book, I will call him 'Mr. Tremaine.'

At home, my stepfather did everything he could to steal my joy. In front of other people, he came across as nice and charming. As soon as my mother and I were home alone with him, he'd find something to get angry about.

Mister Tremaine emotionally and physically abused my mother and I. He made me clean the house repeatedly. I felt like I was Cinderella. I'd end up curled up against the wall with him screaming at me, "You'll never be anything! No one is going to like you because you're black and you have an attitude." This was an everyday occurrence. All I could think in those moments was that he was a liar. God told me otherwise. Mr. Tremaine was a black man himself, and I never understood why he'd say racist things to me.

Thankfully, I was raised to be strong minded, so I wasn't easily influenced by much other than God, my mom, and Mariah Carey. I remember singing every single day after school for the few hours I was home alone, trying to cope with the stress of being a pre-teen and emotionally abused. I studied everything about Mariah. I related to the pain she wrote about in her songs.

I was inspired by her to write metaphorically. I thought if I told the truth about my pains, I'd get in trouble. Mariah's words in songs like "Looking In" were an exact depiction of my life and hit me just as hard as the Bobby Goldsboro song "The Funny Little Clown." My mother instilled in me that I mattered and was valuable, but believing it was easier said than done.

We moved from his apartment to a little house down the street. One night after a surprisingly peaceful dinner, my mother, Mister Tremaine, and I all said goodnight and went to our bedrooms. I changed into my pajamas, hopped into bed, and immediately dozed off. A nightmare chased my sweet dreams away as my subconscious was distracted by distressed-sounding noises coming from my mother's bedroom.

I woke up to my mother screaming for my step-father to leave her alone. Panicking, I grabbed my cell phone and locked myself in the closet. I texted my big sister, *I think he's hurting Mommy!* She lived six hours away, but was actually out of state at the time. My mother continued to yell out "You're hurting me. Stop!" I felt helpless. My big sister called the police and gave them my address.

I thought Mister Tremaine was going to kill my mother that night. When the police came pounding on the door, my mom's screams immediately ceased. I could hear their bedroom door swing open and my step-father's heavy footsteps walking down the hall, headed for the front door. The police questioned Mister Tremaine and insisted on seeing my mother because they received a domestic violence call. Mister Tremaine called my mother out of the bedroom, and she admitted to the police that he was choking her. With visible handprints around her neck, the police told her in front of Mister Tremaine that the only way she could report him or get him taken in, is if she didn't fight back in defense. If she fought back, he could-counter report her. She didn't press charges.

Before that night was over, he screamed and yelled at me for getting my sister involved. He threatened to take away my phone and burn all of my songwriting notebooks. He hated that I wrote everything down. I think he didn't want any documentation of his physical and mental abuse towards my mother and I. Thankfully, my mom refused to let him take or trash any of my personal items. To ensure Mister Tremaine wouldn't get his hands on anything, she turned off my phone and kept it in her purse. She even went as far as taking my notebooks to work with her and locking them away. I remember crying on the bathroom floor that night, talking to God, asking him to save us from Mister Tremaine. I looked into the mirror, knowing that this wasn't how life was supposed to be.

After the police incident, things got even worse for me. Mister Tremaine did everything he possibly could to keep my sister out of our lives and keep us isolated. He would kick my mom and I out of the house, then call her endlessly, wondering where we went. My mother always did what she could to make the best out of bad situations. Mommy and I would go on adventures we'd call *missions*, to the movies and even out of town because of Mister Tremaine's outbursts. We were always in survival mode.

I was a sixth grade honor-roll student, given the nickname 'Preacher' by my peers. I was a mentor and confidant. A natural comforter to others. There was no one to comfort me though. There were times I'd go to school in the same clothes as the day prior. The only new things I'd be sporting, were bruises. One time, my step-father hit me in the face with a belt. My mother wasn't home to protect me.

Somehow, through all the chaos, we dealt with it. These experiences in my life conditioned me to trust no one and to always be leery of men. In spite of all the turmoil, I chose to funnel the pain into productivity. I think that's one of the reasons I'm such a hard worker to this day. I won't wallow for long before finding a way to manifest positivity.

One day, I had a feeling something bad was going to happen. Mister Tremaine was on his way home from work, and I didn't want to be home with him. I was anxious, pacing back and forth in the living room, crying uncontrollably. My mother was sitting on the couch trying to calm me down, but it wasn't working. He pulled into the driveway, and I began begging my mom for us to leave. I remember her eyes tearing up as she watched me, a caged bird, searching for the way out. As soon as he walked in the door, the first thing my mother said was, "We're leaving."

I was scared for our lives as they both began to argue. I knew that I'd kill Mister Tremaine to protect my mother. I didn't care about what happened to me, as long as my mother was safe. My mom quickly went into their bedroom to grab her purse and keys. I rushed into my room to grab my essentials: my bible, a notebook, and a pen.

Everything happened so suddenly. All I can remember was waiting in the living room for my mother, so we could leave. Hearing their arguing get louder was frightening. I could feel the negative energy rising. My mother finally rushed into the living room with Mister Tremaine close behind her heels. They were struggling. I stood by, watching in terror. My mother grabbed a glass of water with her one free hand and threw it against the wall. That must've shocked him because he let her go. My mother then grabbed me, and we rushed to the door. Mister Tremaine slammed the door on the back of my mother's feet on the way out, but we were finally free. I was so relieved to be out of his reach. I wasn't even concerned that we had left all of our belongings. We only lived with my step-father for two years, from my fifth to sixth grade years, but it felt like an eternity.

Within a few days, we looked into getting a storage unit so we could have a place for our belongings. I knew it was only a matter of time before we would run into Mister Tremaine. Sure enough, he happened to pass by the very moment we were asking the storage manager to rent a unit. We informed the storage manager about our situation, and asked if we could park our car inside the storage facility gates behind the building to hide. Thankfully, he said yes.

Shortly after, we were hidden. Mister Tremaine pulled into the parking lot, entered the building, and walked up to the front desk where we had stood only moments before. He asked the manager if a mixed girl and hispanic woman were just there, and the manager said he hadn't seen anyone that fit that description. Mister Tremaine then asked if he could look around, trying for intimidation, but the manager didn't cower to him. After Mister Tremaine left, we got a storage unit. Our next task was to develop a plan to get our belongings out of Mister Tremaine's hell-hole of a house.

One of those nights, we slept at the storage facility in the car. Little did we know, that moment was foreshadowing an experience that would occur over a decade into the future. We eventually went back to the house to find that he had changed the locks. With a new dilemma at hand, we had to come up with a plan to break in while he was at work.

The night we broke into our own house, Mister Tremaine's gun was out on the living room table. There were also a pillow and blanket, as if he slept in there and waited for us to come back. Many questions ran through our minds. What would've happened if we had come to get our belongings when he was home? Would he have shot us? Would he have used the excuse that we were intruders to justify shooting us? We didn't stay long enough to find out. We got all our belongings out and into our storage unit within a matter of hours.

After staying with a few of my mother's co-workers for a while, we moved into a small trailer in the boonies. It had been a few months since we were gone, but Mister Tremaine was working overtime to try to get back with my mom. She was done with him, though. She had filed for divorce.

Mister Tremaine wreaked more havoc since my mother wouldn't take him back. He keyed her car and put flour in our mailbox. Even after their divorce was finalized, he still came around. He had kept the spare key to my mother's vehicle, and would often get in it and move things around just to show he'd been there. Mister Tremaine haunted us like a ghost in a never-ending nightmare. It seemed like no matter how far away we went, that man followed.

We ended up living in the trailer for six months. If you ask me, it was a lot like living on Palm Park Blvd. Insects would crawl into the house from every crevice, and you never knew when the next tornado or storm would throw your belongings into the trees.

Once the lease was up, we immediately moved back to civilization. I finally felt like I had a chance to be somewhat normal.

4

Always Be My Baby

My First Love

My favorite school was just a block away from home. It was the beginning of seventh grade, the year of exploration. I was finally able to be myself without any restrictions. It was a two grade school that only housed seventh and eighth graders. I think having schools with only one or two grades in it is clever. In my opinion, it lowers the chances of bullying and the desire or need to fit in with the older crowd.

I was ecstatic to be in a new place without Mister Tremaine and all the drama he caused by simply existing. I was now finally able to spread my wings. I joined everything: athletics, theater, and drum and piano lessons. I also began performing around town. Mister Tremaine had never allowed me to do extra-curricular activities outside of school, so I took full advantage of my newfound freedom.

Every Friday, I'd hangout at Skateland West with the homies, and was even proclaimed 'Queen of Skateland' before being kicked out. I began the dating, holding hands, talking on the phone all night, and *love* stage of my adolescence. It was bliss, but I had no idea what love meant until I met Dre.

About two weeks into eighth grade, I walked to school like any other day. That day in particular though, I happened to be extra fly. My hair was pin straight, flowing down my back. I was rocking brand-new neon green and baby blue kicks that matched my neon shirt. I walked into the building and headed straight to the cafeteria. I only slowed down to execute a few secret handshakes, then continued on outside to the blacktop.

The only way I can describe what happened next is in this poem I call, "And Then I Saw Him."

It was all ordinary,
Until it wasn't.
Everyone disappeared,
When I saw him.

There he was,
Tall, dark, and handsome,
Gorgeous eyes,
Beautiful smile.

There I was,
Staring,
Awestruck,
Who *is* that guy?
It was love,
Meant to be.
My soul yearned for him.

A blush spread across my face,
My eyes trained on him,
He *would* be mine.

How would it happen?

Through a letter of course.
You interested?
Check yes or no.
He checked yes.

Anticipation,
Waiting to see him,
There he was,
Looking down at me.

"You're not going to say hi to your girlfriend?"
His reply,
A grin and a hug.
We parted for class,
I floated on a cloud.

Later,
Slow motion.
Again, his enticing eyes,
Full of depth and wonder.
"Do you think you could ever fall in love with me?"
Silence in our bubble.
Our bodies one, yet no contact.
His slow grin, "I already have."

Dre and I were inseparable after that. Loving him was easy. Don't get it twisted, he was far from perfect. He was a jokester, like any typical teenage boy. I didn't always think some of the things he did were funny. Making good decisions and hanging out with the best crowd weren't his strengths. Despite that, he never treated me badly. He was actually pretty fun to be around.

I have some fond memories of Dre and I, like the first time he slept over. I know what you're thinking, how in the hell did he get the opportunity to sleep over with his bad boy image and my good girl reputation? I was only fifteen years old to boot. My mother was never a strict parent when it came to stuff like that. When I was little, I think I got spanked a total of three times. That's all it took for me to not test her further.

My mom often used reverse psychology on my sister and I. She'd let us know what she expected of us and trusted that we'd abide by those expectations. Like God does with his children, my mother gave us free will. She gave us free reign to make grown-up choices. If we were to make a compromising decision for ourselves, we'd have to face the consequences. I think that was a great tactic in her parenting skills, because I valued being able to make my own decisions. This helps me with my decision-making process even now.

At that point in my life, I wasn't yet sexually active, but I had a sensuality that with the right person, would want to flow freely. Dre and I had several intimate moments, but he respected that I wanted to save the sexual act for marriage.

The first night he slept over was a night I will never forget because Dre and I took our love beyond the physical. We became one without needing to complete the sexual act. We explored each other through physical touch, kissing, caressing, and meeting each other's needs. It felt natural and was the most intense experience of my life. Though our hormones raged, I knew not to take it further as I wasn't ready for the consequences.

To this day, a lot of my sexual encounters with men in particular, haven't amounted to that. Although we were reeled into each other physically and hungered for intimacy, we controlled ourselves out of respect for one another.

There are many beautiful moments I can recall while being with Dre, from playing basketball after school to writing love notes to each other in our private notebook. Dre was a romantic guy. He'd walk in the pouring rain just to come cuddle and spend the day with me. I was fortunate to experience that kind of love so young. It's something I'll cherish forever.

No other man stood a chance after him. Our relationship spanned two to three years off and on during junior and high school because he ended up leaving me for another girl. My heart was broken, but I gave him a choice between us. He picked her to feed his teenage hormones. Somehow, I still asked for one last kiss.

I cried like a baby. I had broken up with other boys before, but nothing felt more tragic. I thought we could last a lifetime, but couldn't keep him focused on me. I jammed to every Mariah Carey break-up song you could think of, from "Breakdown," to "H.A.T.E.U." Each song expressed the pain I felt trying to get over Dre.

It wasn't easy going through relationship withdrawals. Ninth grade was pretty miserable for me. I was lucky I had extra-curricular activities to keep me busy. I ended up writing enough songs about my heartbreak to make two albums.

Later I tried dating other guys, but those relationships didn't last very long. Dre even tried coming back several times during high school, but we hung with different crowds. While we were apart, Dre's mother passed away. When I heard the news, I broke radio silence to let him know that if he ever needed a friend, I'd be there.

    I still loved him unconditionally. For years, I kept an eye on him. He lost his way after the passing of his mother. To make matters even worse, he also lost his grandmother. His mother and grandmother were the only family he had. They'd always tell him that I was his angel and to never let me go. Since I didn't tolerate his lifestyle and wouldn't let him get back with me, he downward-spiraled even more. I felt for him, but I knew I wasn't going to let anything or anyone come between me and my dreams. I didn't want to allow myself to be content in mediocrity. I channeled everything into my music, dance, or some form of art. I wanted to be productive instead of self-destructive, but it didn't always work. I coped with my growing pains by becoming manipulative, and I took on a much different role from the *good girl* I once was.

5

Mastering Overcoming Boundaries

Becoming an Entrepreneur | Self Discovery | Racism
Concrete Jungle | The Golden Ticket

After Dre, boys hardly mattered to me anymore. I didn't even try to pretend to have feelings for them. I became a player, tossing boys' emotions around like it was a sport. Being popular, I knew I could have anyone I wanted.

I was drawn to manipulating them because I had power and control. I used that ability to get back at all the men that had hurt me up to that point. I'm realizing now, how much bitterness had crept in. No one would've guessed it, just by looking at me.

The twisted thing is that I was honest with the guys. I'd let them know that I was going to fuck with their head, but they were so enamored by me, they didn't care. In the back of my mind, I wanted to make Dre jealous because I still loved him. I relationship-hopped out of boredom with the hope I would get over him.

Underneath it all, I was also hiding the fact that I liked women. Guys were never mature enough to stimulate me mentally, and I was hungering for a connection of the mind. I had significant encounters with girls as far back as third grade. However, because I knew my mother didn't want that for me, I tried to disregard my feelings as a passing phase.

I don't know how no one figured it out sooner. I'd always joke with my friends about being bi-sexual and make bets with the boys to kiss my pretty girlfriends. The longer I tried to fight my desire for women, the stronger it got.

By sixteen, I was performing all over town with the organizations N.Y.A and H.Y.P.E SACADA. H.Y.P.E SACADA stood against drug and alcohol abuse and bullying. Regardless of my inner battles, I was considered a model citizen. I got to perform all over Texas, mentor the youth, be on TV, and write songs for the group. It was a cool time, but I was still trying to get over Dre while fighting off my deepening urge to pursue women.

Every other day after school, I went to dance rehearsals. There was a girl that I was attracted to. I think the fact that she put on this facade that she hated me, drew me into her more. Every time we'd be grouped together to do certain dance routines, I could feel our attraction. Neither of us would've openly admitted it, but by the way she'd look at me, I felt she liked me too.

Trying to suppress my conflicting emotions, I dove into my music. I started production on a concert, while working on my first album, *The Differe[nc]e*. To raise money to fund the album and show, I sold brisket plates and candy at school. I was excited because this show was going to be held at the Carver Theatre and sold on Ticket Master.

I scouted and hired talent to perform with me. I even set up rehearsals to make sure I put together the best show possible. I loved involving people in what I had going on. Giving other people opportunities to shine has always made me happy.

While organizing the production for my concert, my mom ended up finding a better paying job across town. She asked me if I cared that we'd have to move if she took the position. I happily left Southwest to go to Winston Churchill. Southwest was becoming inundated with drama, and I didn't care to be around it any longer. I had a lot going on at the time, and I was desperate for a new beginning.

In the midst of settling into a new school and after months of preparation, it was finally time for my concert at the Carver Theatre. It was amazing that a few hundred people bought tickets and showed up to support me. I was proud of the message I gave at my show. I wrote a whole speech about how, for me, art is not about fame. Being a creative is about being the best example you can be and realizing how impactful you are. The goal is to matter, not to be famous.

After the concert, I finished up my first original album *The Differe[nc]e* and released it on April 27th, 2012. I hosted a private listening party, inviting some old friends from Southwest and a few people I met and connected with at Churchill. Everything during this time was moving at a fast pace. I purposely kept myself preoccupied. I was already well into making my second original album, *New Kinda Feeling*, while involved in new organizations like Rock Star Academy.

My experience at Churchill was one I'd never want to relive. There wasn't much diversity in the school, in the faculty or student body. I tried to find every way possible to stay away from school. I couldn't stand being subjected to the arrogant, one-track minded students that pretended to be all kinds of *woke*.

At seventeen, I was still an AB honor roll student, and taking senior level classes. However, I've never really agreed with the concept of high school. I've always thought that each student should be able to learn at their own pace and about something they're actually interested in. I understand not everyone knows what they want to be early on. For the ones that do, they should be allowed to go to a separate school with like-minded individuals. Having to wait until after high school to get credentials in a specific area of interest seems like a waste of time.

Because I wasn't learning anything I was interested in, I was just going through the motions. I was in a grey area, trying to understand who I really was. I hungered for connection, which always led me back to my biological father.

I think all internal battles have a root cause. Some of us know exactly what causes them, and for others it takes time to learn. I knew some of my struggles had a lot to do with my father. I had bitterness towards my father for not being in my life. I even wrote a whole song about him titled "Nobody" on my first original album *The Differe[nc]e*. I had so many unanswered questions. Writing that song, however, didn't help fill the void.

I brought up to my mother that I needed closure. I also explained to her that I didn't want him to pass away one day without us having had some sort of relationship. I knew that I should and that God wanted me to forgive him, but my emotions held me hostage. I wanted to rub it in his face that I had made it without him.

After lots of research to find out where he currently lived eight or nine years later, we were able to locate a new address for my grandmother. As we approached Abilene before heading on to Lubbock, I felt the weight of resentment and pain lift from me and the excitement of seeing him again settle in. Originally, I had wanted to be ugly towards my father about everything, but God had other plans. I finally felt a sense of peace.

Now that my heart was right, I was ready to once again see my biological father. I was greeted by my uncle James, but the moment with my grandmother Doris was unforgettable. She welcomed me with joy and open arms. I think I got more kisses and hugs in that moment than I had ever gotten in my entire life. It was a beautiful reunion.

Once we woke my dad up from a nap, we were able to catch up together. It was nice to be able to give them all updates about my life and all I was accomplishing. I played him "Nobody," the song I wrote about him. I'll never forget that moment. My mother filmed the whole thing as I watched him listening to every lyric I wrote. That song was my whole heart, and the fact that he was listening to it meant everything to me. His response after hearing it was to cry and say, "It's true. I guess my nickname is 'Nobody' now, huh?"

Words I'll always remember him saying were, "You have a good heart, Natalie. If the shoe were on the other foot, I don't know that I would've looked for my father." I gave credit to my mother, and we said our goodbyes.

Word must've spread that I was in Abilene, because one of my sisters from my father's side gave me a ring while I was in Lubbock. She made sure to let me know that the next time I came into to town, she'd love to see me. After catching up and later bonding over the phone with her, I felt more whole. Knowing your roots is a gift that I think most people take for granted.

Meanwhile, back in school, my junior and senior years were a drag. I was not able to truly be myself at Churchill, as I was always on guard due to the racism I experienced. I didn't take to anyone in particular, other than a few people.

Mid-junior year, I ended up dating a guy I'll call 'Stunt Double' because he was anything and everyone but himself. Our relationship only lasted five months, as we couldn't relate to each other. He was a quiet, funny, mixed guy who seemed cool at first. I soon found out that he was only a gentleman when it benefited *him*. He was materialistic and often rude. I had no idea he was rich, but after spending time with him, I realized I couldn't co-exist in his world. We were just too different. He had no home training.

While we dated, a girl got brought up in our conversations a few times. She was someone he had wanted to date before, but had turned him down. Now that he was tall, muscular, and dating me, he was on her radar.

After we broke up, they got together, and I had to see all of their summer adventures on Facebook. I was happy for them because they seemed like the perfect fit, being materialistic and with no cares in the world. They deserved each other.

During my senior year, the only real downfall was the fact that she was in my last class of the day. Every day she and Stunt Double would make out in front of the class door. It was disgusting. I just wanted to be away from everyone at that school. She often made racist comments in class. All I could think while she would blab on, was how could she be so fucking racist if her boyfriend was half black? All year I managed to be the bigger person, but it sure wasn't easy.

On a more positive note, I became an official auntie a few months shy of graduating. I was technically already an auntie because of my other half sisters, but I didn't get to experience my nieces and nephews from birth. This time I was given the opportunity to be close and have access to someone that was mixed.

I wrote a song for my niece called "It Was like Magic." It featured her cry from the day she was born. My mother and I drove to Sherman from San Antonio to help my big sister the week she gave birth. I can't tell you how much I bonded with that little girl. She fit in just one of my arms, with her head in the palm of my hand and her body extending to my elbow. I've never loved anyone so instantly in my life. She was half white, half hispanic, and I was happy that we shared being mixed. I was relieved that she'd never have to experience what it felt like being half black.

Some would argue that everyone deals with racism, but I don't believe that. People can be mixed and exist with no issues, but if you have one drop of black blood or any black features, you're automatically a walking target. I often tried to explain my bi-racial experience with my big sister, but neither her or her husband could seem to wrap their mind around it. A lot of times I'd try to explain my struggle, it was met with comments like, "What did you do to make them do that to you? Maybe you're too emotional. I just don't understand how anyone would randomly target you." Often times without realizing it, they made remarks that made me feel uncomfortable. Being the little sister, I felt I could never really voice my opinion.

I feel like I battled with my sister and brother in law over their insensitivity to my racial experience for years, until I was twenty-five years old. Things were left unsaid, and I can't really say that if I were to bring it up now, anything would help heal the ongoing battle myself and other black people face daily. You can't make anyone understand something that doesn't affect their lives directly.

My senior year was finally coming to and end. But of course, on the second to last day, someone had to disrupt the peace. It was my last class of the day, the class I shared with Stunt Double's girlfriend. The class was watching a movie, but she and her crew were completely inconsiderate of everyone else trying to enjoy it. I eventually turned around to let her know people were trying to watch the movie, and asked if they could be quieter. I must've struck a nerve, because this girl had the audacity to take a picture of me without my permission, post it on Twitter, and call me a loud, monkey. WTF?

After my friend showed me the tweet, rage filled my entire body and I was so close to kicking her ass. Sure enough, she couldn't help but mumble something else about me under her breath. I immediately got up, enraged, and kicked the chair in front of me. I pushed over the tables that were in my way, and went straight for her. Instead of punishing her, the teacher who had been witness to her bullshit all year, yelled for my friends to remove me from the room. I wondered why was I the one that had to leave when she was the bully and instigator?

I paced the hallways, angry. My homies tried to calm me down, but I couldn't control how upset I was. I ended up walking the few blocks home, frustrated and crying. Once I got to my apartment, I punched a few walls and shattered a glass cup. I hated being upset, so I forced myself to take a nap in an effort to calm down.

My entire body was so sore, that I could barely walk the next day. I know suppressed rage and pain can eat you up inside and cause you bodily harm, so from that day forward, I never allowed myself to reach that point of rage again. If I feel myself ever getting to that point where someone is blatantly disrespecting me or trying to irk me, I immediately remove myself from the situation. Some people are just jerks, and stooping down to their level is never worth it.

I had one more day of school left, and I didn't want to face her again. I asked my favorite of the two black teachers in the school if I could go to her classroom if given permission. Thankfully, my other teacher allowed it, and I was able to end the year on a positive note.

Although my experience at Churchill wasn't the best, I learned a lot. Ignorance and being inconsiderate are learned behaviors that are developed over time. I also learned that just because you have pure intentions, doesn't mean anyone else does. Instead of falling into the cycle of ugliness, choose to love. Equality isn't some unsolvable math equation, it's simple. We all deserve to be treated fairly in the pursuit of happiness no matter our race, gender, etc.

For my graduation gift, my mother got me the one thing I desperately wanted for as long as I could remember: a trip to New York City. I had never asked for much growing up, so New York was a dream come true. I felt at home in Manhattan. The city was exactly like in the movies, lively, with tons of lights and adventures.

I'll never forget the many unexpected things that happened upon our arrival. We walked around exploring, and there happened to be an ASCAP convention being held. Passing by the red carpet, we saw Steven Tyler walk out of his limo and into the building. We tried to sneak in after all the celebrities, but could only get so far. My mother and I were slick enough to get to the entrance of the actual event on the third floor, but the doors were secured and blocked off by two security guards. One guard was kind enough to chat with us about what kind of event was going on inside. We let him know I was a singer- songwriter and also a member of ASCAP. I handed him a rough demo of my second original album, *New Kinda Feeling*, hoping that it would somehow be our magic ticket into the event. Nope.

He did end up giving us information about a bar I could go perform at that night where lots of celebrities watched upcoming talent. My mother and I took the information and caught our first ever subway ride to Ashford & Simpson's Sugar Bar to sign up for open mic night. We arrived just in time for me to get on the list to perform.

I had performed what felt like a million times before that night, but it was special to be able to perform in New York City. It was a small but vibrant bar, jam-packed full of people ready to eat and hear talent. I watched the other acts go on before me, and I could feel my nerves rising from my toes, to my knees, into my stomach, and directly into my heart. When it was finally my turn, I was accompanied by a live band that seemed to be surprised about my song choice of "Nobody's Supposed to be Here" by Deborah Cox. I was a young-looking nineteen year old kid from good ole' Texas, ready to belt out a soulful tune by an amazing vocalist. I knew inside what I was capable of, but the audience had no idea that *sanging* was something I could do.

The musicians began playing. The background vocalists began singing the intro in a two-part harmony. If my mother hadn't recorded the whole thing, I honestly wouldn't have remembered how awesome of a performance it was. All I remember was right before I performed and the aftermath. It was an overwhelming feeling getting a standing ovation. Everyone was asking for how to find me online or keep in touch. I was used to that kind of response in Texas, but knowing New York felt me was an unparalleled feeling. Back in 2013, Instagram was brand-new, so I passed out rough demos of my upcoming album, *New Kinda Feeling*, with my YouTube channel and Facebook information on it.

I can't even remember the ride back to the hotel. My mother and I were ready for bed after such a high. I loved and appreciated moments like that with my mama.

After returning home from New York, I took some time off from school. I contemplated going to college to major in dance and minor in sociology or psychology. I just couldn't picture myself as a college student. After much contemplation, I decided college wasn't for me. I was afraid to break the news to my mother. I didn't know what her response to my decision would be, because it was assumed I'd attend college.

One morning I broke the news to her. I explained to her that I wanted to pursue my music, didn't want to go into debt, and definitely didn't want to study something that I wasn't passionate about. I wanted to use my mind for creativity. I got my mother's blessing to follow my heart, and that's exactly what I did. I remember my mama saying "You can always go back to school, but you'll only be young and able to chase your dreams once. I wouldn't support your decision if I didn't see your talent and truly believe in you."

The following year in January of 2014, my mom told me she wanted to go to beauty school because that was something she'd always dreamt of doing. I cheered her on for making that decision, but somehow she convinced me to register as well. Being in the cosmetology field was never my dream, but I figured I could learn the trade and have a back-up plan.

I invited one of my high school friends to go to beauty school with me. She was smart, but didn't quite know what she wanted to do with her life. I promised her that we'd do it together and would both have a trade under our belt. After several months, during which I had accumulated 508 hours, I realized I didn't want to waste my time anymore. The girl I drove to school everyday had gotten involved with the wrong crowd of girls in beauty school. I was tired of being disrespected by her and confronted her. I let her know I was no longer going to tolerate it. I suggested one of her other friends drive her instead.

I made the decision to no longer attend beauty school. I'm proud to say that the girl and my mother both completed their coursework there. Years later, the girl and I briefly spoke again, and she ended up apologizing for how she behaved while we were in school. We left what happened between us in the past and congratulated each other on our current achievements. The girl is doing well with her cosmetology career now, and I'd like to think I had something to do with that.

Sometime in late 2014, my mother got a phone call about an audition taking place in Austin from an organization called CGTV. The organization was created by Adrian R'Mante, famously known as Esteban Julio Ricardo Montoya de la Rosa Ramirez from a Disney Show I grew up watching called *The Suite Life of Zack & Cody*. I thought it was a scam, but the people kept calling for me to audition, so I finally gave in.

A few days later, we were in Austin. I was asked to do a cold read in front of three judges and two hundred and fifty other auditioning people. I was also asked to show them something I could do that made me special or unique. When I'm asked to do something that makes me special, I sing. I can't remember the first song I chose to sing, but I do remember one of the judges was very *extra* with me. When I say extra, I mean this dude had an attitude and didn't expect me to actually have talent. Once I said I could sing, this judge hit me with "Oh, you sing? Let's hear it. One, Two, Action!" I was prompted to immediately accept his challenge and began to sing.

Everything went silent while my voice resonated throughout the entire conference room. Once I finished singing, I received a standing ovation. The judge made a show of showering me with praises while he marked my audition paper with *Call back! Call back! Number One Pick!* I've dealt with those types of situations all my life. I've always been the underdog, but I'm the type of person that is never afraid to step up to the plate.

Those of us that made the first call-back were told to standby for the rest of the auditioning process. I didn't know what the rest of the audition would entail, but I was excited that I was the 'number one pick'. At the second part of the audition, I was asked to read a new set of lines and to sing. I walked into a different room and immediately saw Phil Lewis, famously known as Mr. Moseby, from *The Suite Life of Zach and Cody*. It was a nostalgic moment for me, but somehow I kept my cool. Mr. Lewis asked me to do a cold read. He was impressed with my memory and ability to make the role I was given believable. I was then asked about any other talents I had, and just like an instant replay, I began to sing. Mr. Lewis was thoroughly impressed. I was given a $2,500 scholarship to Hollywood to take a seven day acting intensive taught by Adrian R'Mante, Phil Lewis, and other celebrity guest mentors.

I made up my mind that I was going to raise whatever other money necessary to attend the week intensive in L.A. and wrap up my 2nd original album, *New Kinda Feeling*. I worked odd jobs at Bowlero and Party City, which was a drag.

While working at Party City, I ran into an old frenemy of mine, the one from H.Y.P.E SACADA. She was the girl who had seemed to hate my guts, yet had given off attraction vibes. I was stocking the shelves, and out of the corner of my eye, there she was. Instead of us giving each other the side eye or, completely ignoring each other, we immediately hugged and began to chat like old girlfriends.

I asked her what she was doing in town, because I'd heard she lived in El Paso. She explained how she was visiting her family with her son for a few days. I was surprised that she had a son, but I congratulated her on her beautiful baby, and we continued to talk. I could feel that we were still physically attracted to each other. I told her we should keep in touch. Without hesitation, she gave me her number, hugged me, and said she had to go but to text her.

After she left, I couldn't get her out of my head. I decided to pursue her. She was resistant at first, for religious reasons, but I persisted. I couldn't get over the fact the girl who used to hate me wanted me. Our casual texts eventually led to more intimate ones. That was the first time I really got to tell a woman how I felt.

I wanted to make what we experienced through the phone reality, but that wouldn't happen until much later. A few months passed. I tried to text her here and there to let her know that I was still interested. At times I'd get lucky enough to get a response from her, but eventually she started a serious relationship with a guy.

It hurt knowing she was getting serious with someone else, but I respected her relationship and let her know I was happy for her. However, I believed we both still wanted each other.

While she was seeing him, I started dating to try and forget about her. I ended up losing my virginity during this time. I was a young adult trying to figure out what I needed from life. The easiest thing to test run at the time, was my sensuality. I wanted to experiment with things I'd never done before. I was tired of reining in my desires for women, and I really wanted to test myself to see what I was really all about. Your twenties are the time to get to know yourself and see what you're capable of. I was so used to doing what I was told and being the *good girl*, that I wanted to test out my bad girl britches. I made the conscious decision to try some weed and entertain some thoughts and ideas I wouldn't normally entertain.

I felt like I was ready for sex, so I tried it. To any young women questioning whether or not to have sex, I'm here to tell you, you aren't missing out on anything. Once you are ready, sex will come naturally when it's supposed to. Your mind, body, soul, and spirit will all be in alignment when it's time. Don't lower you standards, character, or morals for any young punks. Have sex under your own conditions and in your own time.

It wasn't the best experience for me, but I don't regret it. However, I felt like I wasted a beautiful moment on someone I wasn't in a relationship or in love with. I didn't have sex again for over a year after that.

Sometime in December of 2014, I met up with Dre again. He always seemed to find his way back to me, no matter how long it had been. Out of love, Dre and I checked in on each other every so often, but he was living a lifestyle I didn't approve of. I always had to reiterate that he'd never have another chance with me if he continued down that path.

One day Dre and I chilled at my apartment and reminisced. I couldn't help but notice that when I looked into his eyes, he wasn't the guy I had originally fell madly in love with. Dre had a lot of potential, but I was smart enough to know I couldn't change a grown man. All I could do for him was pray, and hope that one day he'd change for himself. In the back of my mind, I felt he'd find his way back to me later in life. Until then, I was content with loving him from afar. I had already lived so many years without him, so I wasn't afraid of letting him go. However, I don't think I'll ever experience the kind of bond him and I shared again in my lifetime. Our love story, was to be continued.

It was now 2015, and I was focused on my relationship with my new boyfriend and finishing my second original album *New Kinda Feeling*. Like with most of my relationships, I wasn't super into him, and it didn't last very long. I felt this guy had an ego, and I just couldn't co-exist with him. Looking back now, I think we tolerated each other because we were musicians, and no one else really understood that lifestyle.

I worked at a call center from January - June of 2015. I took the job to save money for my trip to Hollywood in June and to help with an album listening party I was planning in April, ahead of my album release in May.

Time seemed to be slowing down before my scheduled trip to Hollywood. It was difficult for me to focus at work, when I just wanted to get the hell out of town. I got fired from my job just a few days before I was planning to quit. I had been purposely hanging up the phone, dropping calls for an hour, before my boss rolled up behind me and asked if we could have a chat in her office. She was surprised by my actions, because she knew I was a hard worker.

It was out of my character to be careless, but I just didn't want to be there any longer. Others might call it irresponsible and childish to job-hop the way I often did. I wasn't at work to make it a life-long career. I used those kind of jobs to fund my passions, dreams, and desires. When you know you have a calling for something other than a nine-to-five, everything else is easy to walk away from.

In June, I headed to Hollywood for CGTV. In the program I attended, we were walked through how to audition, handle call-backs, and how to dress. After all of the training, I was prepared for the big showcase at the end of the week. I had such a great time learning from celebrities and getting my first official headshots. Out of everything that happened while I was at the program, my favorite part was getting to perform in front of twenty agents at the famous ACME Comedy Theater with the possibility of getting signed.

The day of the showcase, we rehearsed our scene with our partners. Everyone was talking themselves up, except for me. I try to refrain from being egotistic about my gifts, because it's ultimately God working through me. I know what I'm capable of, I show up, and I execute. I like to observe and be calm before I perform.

Once it was my turn to perform, I had an entrance unlike anyone else's. In rehearsals Adrian R'Mante had recommended I walk and sing from the back of the crowd and onto the stage before my scene. Time flew, and before I knew it, my scene was over. That night I received six callbacks. There was around forty other actors there and about ten of us got at least one callback. I was proud of myself for my performance. It was an experience I'll never forget.

One of my callbacks was from a major agency in L.A., so I scheduled to meet with them while I was still in town. I didn't catch the greatest vibe from that company. Because I didn't live in California, they were reluctant to sign me, so I passed on them. I had five other callbacks to look into, but my mother and I wouldn't be in L.A. any longer than the week we'd initially planned to be there, so we flew back to Texas. I was hoping that by the time I called the other agencies, their offers would still be on the table.

While back in Texas, I officially released my second original album *New Kinda Feeling* on June 27, 2015. I was determined to make a way back to Los Angeles. I told my mother that I wanted to pursue my acting and music career in L.A. She was all for it, so we began to save money to make it happen. We downsized everything, including our apartment, to help save for the big move. The smaller place we ended up getting stuck with was worse than Palm Park Blvd., if you can imagine that. It was moldy and infested with rats and roaches.

The rest of 2015 was a blur. All I can remember was how crappy, scary, and weird living at those apartments was. I just wanted to be in L.A. already. In late November of 2015, I called up the remaining five agencies to see if I could set up meetings with them sometime in December. The only one still interested was The ESI Network.

December rolled around and I flew to L.A. to meet with Nelson, the founder and head manager of The ESI Network. I was intimidated when we first met. Nelson was a no-nonsense kind of person. While he grilled me, I remained calm and made our encounter a simple conversation. You can never go wrong when you treat things like a conversation. In conversations, things happen organically, which helps to take the edge off.

During our meeting, Nelson asked me if I would ever consider moving to L.A. He said it'd be easier to get auditions and take acting classes. I told him that I was already planning to move to Burbank in late January with my mother. I couldn't really tell if he liked me or not because of his poker face. Nelson and I concluded our meeting, and he let me know he was interested in signing me. He said he would love to have a follow-up meeting once I officially moved into town. I was excited and grateful just to have the opportunity for the meeting in the first place.

Heading back home, I was at the airport, about to board. As people de-boarded a plane, I saw Brian McKnight walking out of the gate. He stood directly in front of me. I have never experienced being star struck in my life, but when I saw Mr. McKnight, it was over. I was sitting against the wall facing the boarding area, and I was the only person that recognized him.

With Brian standing directly in front of me I whispered to the girl next to me and said, "That's Brian McKnight." She had no clue who the hell that was. An older woman on the other side of me asked who he was, because she could see how I was struggling to keep my composure. After I told her who he was, she pretended to know exactly who I was talking about. I leaned over to the girl beside me and asked if she would take a picture of him and I.

I have no idea how I had the ability to stay outwardly calm and collected, because on the inside, I was completely losing it. My adrenaline was on a million. I walked up to him, told him I was a singer and huge fan, then I asked him for a picture. He graciously took the picture with me, and I floated to heaven.

I made sure that I posted that I had met Brian McKnight on social media, then I texted everyone the picture of us before I had to put my phone on airplane mode. After I landed in Arizona for my connecting flight to San Antonio, I noticed that he had retweeted our picture together. That made my day even better.

In early January of 2016, my mother and I continued to aggressively save money for our big move. We sold pretty much everything we owned. It was finally time to leave San Antonio behind and have a new beginning. I couldn't wait!

6

The Great Escape

On January 28th, 2016, we packed up our cars and drove to California. I felt I needed a major life change to help myself change. I didn't want to be manipulative anymore. I thought moving to Cali would help. What I soon found out was that location doesn't change what's inside of you. It's a daily battle to be the person that you want to be.

I remember seeing all of the cars flying by on the highway with the mountains in the background. Being new to California, we didn't know how unbearable the heat could be during the day, or how cold it could get at night. After settling in to our new apartment, I met up with The ESI Network on February 1st, 2016 to officially become an actress on their roster. I then began a month-long pilot program with CGTV that started on February 2nd.

The money my mother and I had saved to get to L.A. depleted fairly quickly. We had to register our vehicles, and were charged $2,000 plus for each car to be registered and smog tested. In retrospect, if we could've foreseen what was going to happen to us, we wouldn't have registered both cars. I would've just registered mine so I could legally be a part time Uber driver, but we were law abiding citizens.

The pilot program began. It was full of audition techniques that prepared each actor for any kind of situation that could occur while in an audition. I also had the privilege of meeting stars, such as RJ Cyler and Tyler Steelman. After the pilot program, I went on tons of auditions to wet my feet and get used to the process.

One of my first auditions, while living in California, took place on March 2nd, 2016. I drove all the way to Northridge from Burbank to a college called CSUN. I auditioned for some students that were making a short film project titled *Homesick*. I felt it went how a typical audition should go. Apparently I did a good job, because two days after the audition, I received a callback that I got the role. I was then sent an itinerary for table reads and rehearsals before officially filming on the CSUN campus. I was excited for the role opportunity and couldn't wait to see how it would all play out. Going to rehearsals was fun and laid back. After all the required table reads and rehearsals, it was time to film *Homesick*. Opportunities like that, prepare actors for other auditions by giving them the ability to see what it's like to be on a set.

I was hyped about all that I was able to get involved with in California. Everything felt hopeful again. Little did I know, I was on the cusp of even more life-changing experiences and events.

While exploring my acting, music, and being an Uber driver, I was also unburying personal triggers I had yet to fully overcome. My goal was to be less self-destructive and grow out of whatever I was still holding onto in my mind. I have to give myself credit for being self-aware when I'm wrong. I know I need to make changes within myself when I get too negative or am operating from the wrong place.

Prior to moving to Burbank, I had discovered many of my triggers and was continuously working on them. I was proud that I'd gotten so far with my personal growth, but I still had many more mental obstacles to break through. One trigger I had was confusion about why my dad wasn't around. I feel I manipulated and caused confusion for other guys because my dad and cousin did that to me. That was my biggest downfall.

During this time of self-improvement, a highlight in my life, was I got to attend my first ASCAP convention on April 27th, 2016. At the convention, you get to network, attend sessions to learn how to capitalize on your music career. You also get to be around celebrity guests. That year, Brian McKnight happened to be in attendance. I had the privilege of seeing him perform. After a long day of seminars and note-taking, hearing Brian McKnight sing was icing on the cake.

After the show, I waited outside in the front, and saw Brian McKnight walking directly towards me. I didn't know if he'd recognize me from the airport, but I had a lot more courage to make casual conversation with him this time around. I let him know that his performance was wonderful and it was a pleasure to see him again. Brian said he remembered me from the airport a few months back. I was happy that he hadn't forgotten me.

Not too long after attending the ASCAP event, other opportunities arose with celebrities who stumbled upon me. Pusharod, who discovered rapper YG, was interested in working with me. I found that none of them seemed to have a game plan though. There was always a lot of talk of how they could help me. They'd work with me as long as I was willing to put in work and do what I was told without asking questions about the process. I've never been the type of person to just trust someone's word without seeing any action.

I despise empty promises, people wasting my time, and being played with. Unfortunately, I crossed paths with many who had no follow-through or who wanted to work with me for all the wrong reasons. I was targeted by men who were supposed to guide, lead, and be an example. They abused their power by trying to manipulate me for their own satisfaction and gain. I was offended by those encounters. I'm a woman that likes to use my brain, work hard for what I deserve, and not sleep my way to the top. Although, I probably would've had a much easier life, if I had used my looks to my advantage. I wouldn't have been able to sleep at night, however, knowing I was insulting my own intelligence by making myself small for an opportunity.

I purposely avoided those types of situations, even if it meant that it'd take me longer to make my dreams a reality. I would much rather have my dignity and respect than compromise my morality. All those encounters were small hiccups considering the reality I would soon face while striving for my dreams.

I turned twenty-two on September 17th, 2016. Around that same time, my mother was having issues with the company she was working remotely for that was stationed in Texas. Her work hours kept being cut, and her employers would declare days off with no notice. California is not the place to be short on rent or bills. My mom searched for a second job to supplement her income and found a computer software company she could work for part time on commission. Every day, my mother would work from 5:00 - 6:00 am at her first job, drive to her second job and work from 7:00 am - 3:00 pm, then drive back home and work for the first job from 4:00 pm - 11:00 pm.

One morning while driving to her second job, my mom put on the Christian radio station that aired different pastors' sermons during her commute. One of the pastors she gravitated to during her forty-five minute drive was Pastor Paul Sheppard. Every day Pastor Paul gave a sermon, and my mother raved about him to me. She told me to listen in, because it felt like his sermons were tailored for us. While working long hours Uber-ing for hardly any pay, auditioning for roles, and taking acting classes, I began to listen to Pastor Paul as well. I found out he had an app called Destined for Victory where you could listen to all of his sermons. Pastor Paul was a God-send, and he seemed to be a confirmation that everything would be okay if we stayed diligent and focused.

It felt tacky how my mother's job was treating her, considering how much money she brought in to the company. Eventually, she had enough of their bull when her work ethic and integrity were questioned. Her employers had the audacity to call her work *shabby* after my mother questioned why her hours were being cut. Overwhelmed and under-appreciated, my mother decided to clock out for the last time while she still had her dignity intact.

One night during dinner, my mother and I came to the conclusion that being homeless was our only option moving forward. My mother and I knew God had sent us to California for a reason. We felt that if we went back to Texas at that point, it would've been like I was giving up on my calling.

We began strategically planning how we'd go about living out of our cars. I came up with the idea of laying down our back seats and using towels and foam so it would be like a mini bed for us. My mother and I are only about five-two, so our bodies would fit perfectly.

I believe we were led by God and were equipped with natural survival skills. We took many precautions to make sure we wouldn't be noticed while in the car, and that we would be as comfortable as we could be. We cut up a black shower curtain to block every tinted window to be sure no one could see inside the vehicle. On one of our trial-run nights, it was chilly, so we knew our regular blankets wouldn't be enough to keep us warm. We added sleeping bags to keep us warm on the cold nights.

A week or so before we made it official to live out of the car, my mother heard on the radio that Pastor Paul Sheppard would be in Glendale, California. Glendale was around thirty minutes away from us, so we decided to be there.

Meeting and taking a picture with Pastor Paul was a highlight during that time, because we knew what we were about to dive into. Not more than a month later, we were officially homeless and living out of our cars. It felt like God sent Pastor Paul to comfort us through his weekly sermons.

7

Homeless For The Calling

All of our non-essential apartment belongings were now in a storage unit. My mother and I got a membership at a 24 Hour Fitness and found a somewhat safe place nearby to park our cars when it was time to go to sleep. We developed a routine for our daily necessities.

On weekdays we'd wake up at 3:30 a.m. to be at the gym by 4. My mother and I would gather what we needed to get ready for the day from her trunk. We'd shower at the gym, grab a small breakfast from McDonald's, and be off to work by 7 a.m. I'd sometimes climb into her backseat and nap or write until she got out of work around 3 p.m. At her job, she could park in a shaded parking garage. That was the coolest place for me to catch up on sleep if I needed it.

On Tuesdays, we'd go to the laundromat to wash our clothes. Due to limited space, we only carried a week's worth of clothes in the car. We kept a small backpack to store non-perishable foods like Vienna sausage, crackers, and chips.

On weekends, my mother and I slept in as long as we could before the sun or too many people out and about forced us to wake up. Some people might think that homeless people have fewer things to do, less worries, and can get all the rest they need. That couldn't be further from the truth. You have more to do than the average person who lives in a house, because you no longer have the luxury of lounging about in your home after work. My mother and I had to constantly find places to hide, park, and stay out of the heat like under a covered parking lot of a local mall.

We didn't have money to waste, so we only spent forty bucks a week on groceries and shared a weekly burger and fries at Denny's to break the monotony. We still had regular bills like our two car payments, the storage unit, the gym cost, and our phone bills. When I look back at all that we juggled, I applaud us for our resilience and strength to endure. We were lucky we had each other during that trying time.

On Thanksgiving Day, we went to our storage unit to clean out our car and check on our belongings. We saw two older women trying to tie down a table on top of their car. My mother and I have a knack for making things fit in tight spaces. We're real-life Tetris experts. After seeing them struggling, we offered to help and had their table securely tied onto their vehicle in no time.

Our original plan after situating our stuff at the storage unit, was for my mother and I to go to feed the homeless including ourselves. However, the two ladies invited us to their Thanksgiving gathering instead. We kindly declined saying it was out of the way from where we lived, but both women insisted on us going. They let us know what time dinner would be and said that the door would be open. After running some errands, we couldn't find a reason not to go, so we made our way to their home in Compton.

We turned into the neighborhood and found that it was nothing like we had thought it would be. It looked like a scene from a movie with palm trees, wide roads, and cute houses. Everyone I'd ever heard talk about Compton made it out to be hood and dangerous. What I saw and experienced was a true community of people that were family-oriented. We parked in front of their lovely home and made our way inside. My mother and I were welcomed with open arms, and we ended up helping out in the kitchen as if we were family. It was nice to feel normal for a bit and to be in good company. God orchestrated it so perfectly for us to not have to spend Thanksgiving alone.

Many people stopped in for the festivities, but I connected with one guy in particular. A few months after that encounter, he ended up taking me on a date. I let him know on our date that my mother and I were homeless. I made it clear that I wasn't looking for any help, that it was just something I was going through. He was kind and understanding about my situation, and he didn't pity me or make me feel weird for telling him. From time to time, he would check in on me to see how I was doing and we'd have a simple conversation. It was nice having someone to talk to every now and again.

At one point, our texts got a little saucy and he convinced me to come see him. I was vulnerable and gave into the hunger for normalcy more than intimacy. Once I arrived, he walked me in and everything was exactly how he said it would be: innocent and sweet. Until my hormones and vulnerability got the best of me, that is. I went back to be with him at least once a week, if not more. He was the only thing I felt I could dive into with no strings attached. Being with him also gave me the chance to be normal for a few hours.

There were other times that were probably more therapeutic for me than just fulfilling a physical need. A lot of the time, I climbed into the backseat of my car, after a day of Uber-ing or auditioning, and just spent time thinking. I had a lot of time to sit with myself and dissect the things floating around in my mind. My process was to write. I didn't just write music, I wrote scripts and even started a vlog titled *Homeless For The Calling*. Through those outlets, I got rid of internal trauma I didn't even realize I was still dealing with.

I wanted to inspire people watching me to never give up, no matter what obstacles they faced. I didn't want to cover up my reality, so lying about my situation was out of the question. Plus, it was nice to have something to keep me busy in the hours I wasn't working or looking for shade.

One day while scheduling episodes of *Homeless for the Calling* on YouTube, I stumbled upon an opportunity in the comments section of one of my viral videos titled "Father Can You Hear Me?" I was asked to sing at a wedding that happened to be located in California. I checked the date it was initially posted, and saw that it had only been posted a few hours earlier. I told my mother about the opportunity and emailed the commenter about his inquiry. I was offered $250 to sing with him at his wedding as a surprise to his wife, who absolutely loved that song from Tyler Perry's movie *Diary of a Mad Black Woman*. I feel it was ordained that I was in California and able to attend and perform at the wedding. It was a beautiful moment forever documented in my *Homeless for the Calling* series on YouTube.

Throughout the time that I was homeless, God showed up in the most unexpected ways. While premiering my YouTube series, I was cast as a well-paid extra for a movie called *Unicorn Store*. I happened upon the opportunity by being an extra through Central Casting. I needed the money, and was given free breakfast, lunch and dinner. While on set, I often met cool people and networked, so I couldn't pass that up.

After a long day on the set in December, Nick Cannon was on a Facebook live talking about his new EP *The Gospel of Ike Turn Up*, through which he allegedly spoke about his relationship with his ex-wife Mariah Carey. Because of his involvement with Mariah Carey, I kept track of what he was doing. As a true lamb, I was trying to make sure he wasn't going to talk shit about my girl Mariah.

I hopped onto Facebook and heard him mention something about discovering and working with upcoming artists. At that moment, I repeatedly asked in the comments about the process for auditioning. My question was finally read and answered by Nick. I thanked him on Twitter for answering my question, and he followed me. In response to him following me, I flooded my Twitter with tons of covers and original music to see if he'd notice or comment, but it didn't seem to work. After that, I went about my days and kind of forgot about the whole Nick Cannon answering my question thing.

8

Overdue

June Gloom | Rise and Shine | The Associate

Most people are aware of how lovely the days are in California, except for the month of June. This chapter of my life reminds me of what Californians call 'June Gloom' because it's a big grey area. You can think something shows up in your life for one reason, only to find that it leads you onto an entirely different road.

On January 14th, 2017, while scrolling through Twitter, I saw a retweet from Nick Cannon. In the retweet, it said he was still looking for submissions for some sort of challenge he launched in late December. Feeling that God wanted me to jump on the opportunity, I woke my mother up and told her we had to go to the gym to shower so I could audition. For the challenge, I had to write a verse to one of Nick's songs on SoundCloud and submit it through social media.

I filmed my audition on my phone in the backseat of my mother's car. After a few takes, I tried to edit what I'd filmed on my laptop, but found I couldn't as it was live. Everyone else who had auditioned submitted pre-recorded audios and professionally recorded videos. I was devastated that I couldn't edit my video, but I submitted it and hoped for the best.

Nick retweeted my submission the next day, and I flipped out, feeling like I might win. My mother romanticized the whole situation, insinuating that Nick might be the key to me making it due to all the platforms he had at his disposal. Something in me felt otherwise. I didn't expect him to ever *make* me, but I did expect a fair opportunity. I wanted a chance to show what I could bring to the table through my work ethic.

After a week, I was asked for my number by a guy in Nick's camp. I'll call this guy 'The Associate.' After researching him and verifying who he was, I gave him my number. A couple of days later, a call came in from who I thought was The Associate. He told me Nick really liked my submission, and to put that number in my contacts so we could stay in touch. My mother and I both cried, feeling like God's plan was unfolding before us. We then went for a walk to reflect on what happened and how it could change our lives. I was still a bit skeptical of it all. I was grateful for the possibility, but I felt like God was letting me know that while this was a cool moment, it wasn't *the* moment.

I don't tend to jump to conclusions because nothing is ever really what it seems. Not to sound negative, but you always have to be cautious about people's intentions and the logistics before blindly trusting. A few months passed, and I was in the top four out of thousands of submissions. I was excited and patiently anticipated what was to come.

All the while, both my mother and I continued to work. I got contacted by my friend Isaac Miller, director and writer of *Homesick*, a short film I was cast in a year prior. He called to see what I was currently up to. I informed him of my situation and how I was in a challenge involving Nick Cannon.

Isaac had originally reached out to me because he remembered how my mother and I had sold everything we owned to move to California. He thought that was inspiring enough to film a documentary about. Now that we were homeless and I was in a contest for Nick, he felt it would sweeten his proposal to his new film crew for their final thesis in film school. I met with Isaac and the crew's producer about the idea of doing my story, and he was awestruck. I remember him saying, "It feels like the stars are aligning for you." He thought I was the perfect subject for their thesis.

Once the crew got to know me, they were all sold on my story and decided to move forward with the filming of *Rise and Shine*, the documentary about my journey of being homeless in L.A. From March 25th through April 27th of 2017, my mother and I were followed and filmed by the crew.

During that time, I was still in contact with Nick's people, anticipating the outcome of the contest. My mother and I were starting to grow tired of living out of our cars. The only reason we stayed in California as long as we did, was because the documentary was going to premiere on Mother's Day at the Writer's Guild in Beverly Hills, and I was still in the running for Nick's challenge. For the premiere, I invited my acting manager Nelson Paredez-Parks, Nick Cannon, and The Associate he often had me in contact with. My mother and I got dolled up for event at the gym. Once there, we walked up and down the red carpet together taking pictures with our *Rise and Shine* movie poster, then headed into the theater. Nick and The Associate didn't end up making it to the event, but Nelson did.

The theater was nearly full to capacity with directors, editors, subjects, actors, managers, etc. Each short film created by the Northridge CSUN students was played. There were several categories, so we had the privilege of seeing multiple bodies of work before watching our own. Prior to *Rise and Shine* being shown, I sat in my chair wondering how it would be received. I hoped that it would be inspiring and allow people to realize that you don't have to literally wear your struggles on your sleeves. It is more of a state of mind. I was still homeless at the premiere, but no one would have ever guessed that by simply looking at me.

Gauging by everyone's expressions witnessing the documentation of such a pivotal moment of my life, I felt an overwhelming sense of compassion rising in the theater. The final scene played and the credits ran, and a moment of stillness filled the room. It was followed by a roaring standing ovation. I was so proud to be able to share that moment with my mama on Mother's Day. The film was nominated best documentary and won best directing. I couldn't have been more grateful. My mother and manager stood on both sides of me and cried. I just took it all in. It was one of those moments I knew made God proud.

Afterwards, everyone gathered in the conference area where we mingled, took pictures and chatted about all the films we had just watched. I floated around the room being asked all kinds of questions about my homelessness, but the one question I remember most was from my manager. "What is it that keeps you going?" My answer can be found in this poem.

Endure

I endure by faith.
God has the ultimate plan for me,
He is everlasting,
I can trust His plan in my life.
I can overcome any trial I face,
I am anointed and highly favored,
God works through me,
Giving me peace,
Beyond all understanding.

After the night was over, my mama asked me "You know what I would have done if I would've known we were going to be homeless?" I asked what, and she said, "I would've bought a van." It's those kinds of moments that truly make me appreciate my mama. I know I've gotten as far as I have because she has always believed in me and has always trusted that I wouldn't waste any genuine opportunity given to me. Besides God, my mama is the only person who has been with me all my life. It's the greatest feeling in the world to know you have someone that'll ride with you through absolutely anything.

Although being homeless was rough, ordinary moments with my mother were special. I cherished every moment with my mother, and even though she's far from perfect, I wouldn't have chosen to endure that hardship with anyone else. From doing our taxes at the public library, to selling stuff out of our storage unit for extra money, my mother and I were continually mastering overcoming boundaries.

Thank you Mommy. I love you.

During this time I was still able to function on a daily basis, but my mental state was fragile. I was constantly on guard and in survival mode. My mind was stretched to capacity, like a rubber band, ready to break at any minute.

I was still in contact with Nick's associate, every now and then. I felt like I was being toyed with. He'd contact me to see if I was free to meet up, then wouldn't hit me back until the next day. I take professionalism and first impressions seriously. I hadn't even met the man, and I wasn't catching the best vibe.

I had been keeping an eye out for updates about the challenge on social media, but of all the posts I saw, none were about the challenge. This kept all the contestants wondering and asking questions. In late May of 2017, I was told I *basically* won the challenge. They never really made an official announcement, but abruptly ended the contest, and started saying I was the new NCredible R&B Princess. They even claimed I was signed, although no contracts were ever involved. Since I knew that I'd *basically* won, my mother and I figured we could probably get back to Texas soon.

By mid-June, I let Nick's associate know I was planning on going back to Texas by July. Soon after that, he invited me to attend a premiere of Nick Cannon's new movie in late June. Once the movie was over, my mother and I watched everyone taking pictures with Nick from a distance and patiently waited to meet him. Once we approached him, we snapped a few pics. He said it was great to finally meet me, and that we had to get into the studio to cook up soon. Meeting Nick was nothing like meeting Brian McKnight. He seemed so regular.

Eventually, we had a meeting with Nick and his gang at a recording studio in Burbank. I was asked a lot of questions about how I got to L.A., and what I looked to do involving my music career. I let everyone in the room know what a hard worker I was, and that I had a huge catalog I was more than ready to share with the world. I stated that my mother and I were still homeless, and we were looking to go back to Texas to get back on our feet. I played them some records. Everyone, including Nick, seemed touched by our story.

I was asked if I was a patient artist that would be loyal to the gang. Being focused and down for someone who was down for me, was important. I whole-heartedly believed that something awesome would come of us working together, given the numerous platforms Nick had at his disposal and with how he said he would" Change my life."

While in our meeting, Nick didn't hesitate to mention how he discovered and helped other acts like the New Boys, Kehlani, and even H.E.R. He claimed their business relationships were short-lived due to them branching out on their own and not being loyal or focused on what his camp had planned for them. I knew that I was a hard worker. If it came down to it, I'd excel in whatever tasks were set before me.

Out of nowhere, Nick offered to have my mother's car shipped to Texas, to fly her home, and have me put up in my own apartment with a monthly allowance, so I could be a full-time musician. Feeling excited at hearing his plans for me, I couldn't wait to begin working.

Nick and The Associate told me to start apartment-hunting, so my mother and I got on it. We found an affordable studio apartment under the $1,000 budget that Nick gave us. Everything seemed to be running smoothly, until reality hit us. My mother and I couldn't put anything in our name since we'd broken our lease and owed more than $5,000 in rent. We were stuck with the options of having to pay off that debt, which we still didn't have, or we would have to have someone sign for us. We brought up the dilemma to The Associate and Nick, and they came back with the solution of putting it in one of their names. Thinking we were all set, we were ready to move forward, but The Associate kept holding off.

We eventually ended up having another meeting with The Associate without Nick around, and he didn't want to revisit what Nick had initially offered us. Since it was clear that we weren't going to get the apartment, my mother and I asked if we could at least have a place to stay for five days. That way we could retrieve our belongings out of the storage and load them into our cars to be shipped back home to Texas.

Once we brought that up, The Associate replied with, "Shipping a car?" Dumb-founded, we once again brought up what Nick offered us in the last meeting we all had attended, but The Associate said he couldn't recall.

He reneged everything that was initially offered to us. He told us he was in charge, and that everything had to go through him before Nick. We reiterated that we needed a place to stay for five days so we could organize and get back to Texas. The Associate finally agreed to let us stay in one of Nick's mansions in Calabasas, California. We soon learned that even if we had been told things would go one way by Nick, they usually didn't end up happening, due to what we felt was The Associate's interference. My mother and I weren't looking for any handouts, we just wanted to get our lives back together.

Once at the mansion, The Associate gave us a tour of each floor. He put us in the room right next to the master bedroom where he stayed for a few of the days that we were there, claiming that the house was *basically* his. In the five days that my mother and I stayed in the mansion, we were probably more uncomfortable there than we ever were sleeping in our cars. I've never lost respect for someone so quickly before in my life. I was disgusted being around him and his half-clad girls that were around my age. He was old enough to be my dad! He could never look me in my eyes. That should have been a huge red flag.

We were still homeless at the time, and didn't have much money for travel. In spite of all the unfulfilled promises, I somehow still had the courage to ask for a little money for our long drive home to Texas. Nick approved it, but The Associate tried to keep it from us. The following quote comes to mind when I think about this entire situation.

"When someone shows you who they are, believe them the first time." - Maya Angelou

I was told to leave my car, full of all of my stuff, at the mansion until I came back to L.A. I was also told that I'd be set up somewhat like Kehlani, who Nick had discovered and helped out at the beginning of her career. Nick and his camp constantly compared me to Kehlani, as if I was some sort of replica of her.

While my mother and I packed our things into her car, The Associate watched us without once offering to help. He claimed he hadn't done manual labor in over a decade, and he wouldn't lift a finger. I couldn't wait to be out of The Associate's presence, but I was nervous to leave my car at that house.

It was the scariest experience being on the road and in a car full to capacity. We barely had room for ourselves. Imagine the mid-July heat, not having car insurance, having all your belongings stuffed into black trash bags, while having to cross state borders with cops at every turn. So many things could have went wrong on that journey. Thankfully we got to Texas safely, and headed straight for my sister's house.

Initially, I think my sister was happy to have us around and no longer homeless. After some time passed, I felt like she was more happy to have my mother around than me. I can't speak for my sister or my brother-in-law, but at the time I felt a lot of animosity coming from both of them, and I didn't really understand why. I was often questioned about why Nick couldn't pay for my mother's and my stay at my sister's home. After she found a job, my mother payed what she could afford to pay. They often asked questions my mother and I just didn't have the answers for. I feel this caused inaccurate assumptions to be made. I often purposely isolated myself. I felt pressured to create a result, involving my career, that I had no control over at the time.

My mother and I didn't expect to stay at my sister's house as long as we did, but that's what it came to. Nick and The Associate said they wanted me back in L.A., but I ended up staying in Texas until early October of 2017. It seemed like forever. I was ready to get to work. I felt compelled to prove to everyone that my life's pursuit wasn't a waste of time. Every day that I wasn't able to create or be myself, it seemed like my dream was withering away.

Even though I technically wasn't homeless anymore, the mentality of being homeless hadn't worn off yet. Nick Cannon's approaching birthday on October eighth, reminded me of Dre's birthday on the ninth. I was in a vulnerable state, craving some sort of familiarity, so I texted Dre to wish him a happy birthday. Even if we're not together romantically, I'll always love him. We've developed a habit of checking on each other from time to time. He didn't fail to make me laugh and smile, but I still felt alone. This was supposed to be a beautiful time in my life, being discovered by someone famous. I didn't feel the joy I should've been feeling. The waiting game was brutal. It was like I was being ripped apart, piece by piece, and no one could tell.

On October 12th, Nick flew me to New York City to record some vocals for a project he was working on called 'Model Music.' During my stay, I was asked to recite a poem and sing a few ad-libs. Most of the time though, we just listened to music. I was flown back to Texas, only to wait some more, and fall into an even deeper depression.

When things aren't going right, my reflex is to stay busy. The problem with this, is that no one can ever tell when I'm good or when I'm overwhelmed and hurting. I tried to keep myself busy by creating YouTube videos, writing new songs, and performing in Dallas. However, the more I tried to pretend everything was peachy, I was losing more and more of myself.

I had a constant feeling of uncertainty and confusion about the whole situation with Nick and his team, because I kept being told one thing and shown another. Up to that point in my life, I had been through what I felt were more trying times, so I didn't feel like I had the right to be so mentally unstable. I was supposed to be dealing with people that were there to help, not cause more difficulties. I prayed everyday. I asked God to reveal to me what I needed to do in this situation, and how I needed to react or operate. I fought with myself daily, trying to figure out why this blessing felt so wrong. The whole time I dealt with Nick's team, I didn't know whether to cooperate or walk away. God was revealing exactly what I needed to do, but because I gave his team the benefit of the doubt, I stayed around longer than I should've.

I flew myself back to L.A. to supposedly be set up like Kehlani and be able to work. Once again, The Associate didn't allow that. For reasons I'll never understand, I feel like he purposefully made things complicated for me. Once I landed, I headed to the mansion to go pick up my car. The Associate knew exactly when I'd arrive to get my car, but he told me that he was about to go to a party. I was already mentally drained, and that made me feel attacked.

I was forced to call Nick to get some sort of cooperation while trying to get my vehicle. I was upset about the whole situation, because I'd planned this weeks in advance with little to no money. Nick was concerned about the situation, and he called his bodyguard to the mansion to help me get my car. After we left, I was then told to follow the bodyguard to another mansion in the hills near Hollywood. The new place was also Nick's house, but he had a young lady living there a majority of the time. Maybe they thought me being around her would make things easier while I was in transition for whatever they did or didn't have planned for me.

I had expiring license plates, a car full of everything I owned, no money, and no real place to be. The girl they had me with was nice, but she wasn't someone I wanted to hang out with. I was put in the guest house beneath the mansion, which felt like a dungeon. I felt hopeless and misunderstood, and there was no one for me to talk to. The only people I saw were Nick's bodyguard or his engineer and even then, only twice.

I let the bodyguard know my concerns about my license plates being expired, and that I was afraid it'd be towed with all my belongings in it. He gave me custom license plates, and I appreciated the gesture. However, I still didn't feel safe driving around in a car full of everything I owned. I took everything out of it and carried it down the two flights of stairs into the guest house. Since I had some time on my hands, I reorganized everything I owned and got rid of some stuff. I wanted to make it easier on myself if I had to haul everything to a new location.

I had been repeatedly asking for the studio time I'd been promised. It sucked having to beg to work. On November 15th, 2017, I recorded the song "Overdue," featuring Nick Cannon. Being in the studio is like a dove flying in the wind, effortless and smooth. I love recording and arranging music, so knocking out "Overdue" was a piece of cake.

Since I wasn't allowed to do much else in the studio, I asked if I could go back home for Thanksgiving. Thankfully, Nick flew me home to spend the holiday with my mom. I got stuck in Texas again, for much longer than I had intended. December was right around the corner. I didn't like that I was, once again, away from all of my belongings. Since I was still talking to Dre on and off, I asked him to help me go get my car from L.A. I promised him I'd pay him back once I got my car back to Texas, and was able to be an Uber driver again. He seemed like he really wanted to help me out, and even rekindle our old flame, but something in me knew it was too good to be true. Dre and I ended up getting into an argument, so I asked my aunt to borrow money for a ticket to L.A. I was afraid to go to California alone, and it sucked feeling like I couldn't count on anyone to be there for me.

Throughout this time, I was having suicidal thoughts. I felt like nothing was going right for me, and I had a strong sense of hopelessness. Once I arrived to Cali, I stayed long enough to get a little funds from Nick to make sure I could get back to Texas. I was finally given a little cash on December 2nd, so I immediately loaded up my car with my belongings. I didn't want to be on the road during winter storms. While packing up in the house, I looked outside one last time and noticed that the moon looked peculiar and bigger than usual. I didn't look too far into it, because my main focus was to get back home in one piece.

Little did I know, the day I chose to drive home on December 3rd of 2017, there was a supermoon event. That supermoon won't happen again until I turn fifty-three, the same age as my mother the year of my long journey home. The drive was empty, the dark sky illuminated by the huge Moon. Once I got out of the state, I sped, trying to beat the sunrise. I only stopped a few times for necessities and a quick thirty minute nap. I was jittery from too many energy drinks and afraid of the possibility of hitting wild animals. I knew I was too exhausted to be able to dodge them if they did appear. Upon returning home, it took me about three days of sleeping to recoup from that twenty-one hour drive. I don't know how truck drivers do that for a living. Back in Texas, I just wanted to disappear. As depressed as I was, I don't remember all that went on. It was a dark time for me, and I don't care to revisit it all that much.

On January 14th, of 2018, I was flown to L.A. to record. I ended up recording "Simple," a song written by Dialo that was given to me by Nick Cannon. I featured on a song called "Fuck Him" by Nick Cannon, off of his *Fuck Him Trilogy* project. I wasn't in L.A. very long, but while I was there, I recall meeting a lot of people that had similar stories to mine. It intrigued me how many artists had been in Nick's camp for several years and had yet to achieve success.

Periodically, I tried to check in with Dre. I didn't get any responses, which was unusual. I had several conversations with my mother about what may have happened to him, and we both grew suspicious and concerned. I sensed that he needed help, I just didn't know with what. Meanwhile, things seemed to be moving a little faster regarding my music, so I went with the flow and tried to stay focused on that.

On April 6th, 2018, "Fuck Him" officially released. Then on April 15, 2018, "Simple" dropped as well. I was so excited. It seemed like everything Nick told me would happen, was finally happening. Nick said my EP would also be coming out soon, and all he had to do was push the button for it to go. As far as press went, all that happened was a photoshoot and he booked two interviews, one of which never saw the light of day.

In trying to cause a buzz, I had people all over the world making videos singing and jamming to my song. Family members, people from school, and some of my celebrity friends showed love. Nick even posted a clip of the song on his Instagram story, which caused frenzy.

I only had twenty-five monthly listeners on Spotify and less than 1,000 streams on my record, in spite of all my efforts. The Associate said he knew how to do a proper rollout, and would cause a buzz for my releases, but that never happened. It was sad being held on a string, thinking something would come from our business relationship. The more time that passed, I became more discouraged being involved with them.

     Sometime in August of 2018, I found out from an old high school friend that Dre was in jail. He couldn't disclose too much information at the time because it was an open case, but he said Dre was convicted of murder. I couldn't believe what he was saying. Dre would never kill anyone unless it was self defense. Concerned, I asked for Dre's information to write to him. I wrote Dre a letter to see if he was okay. I also wanted to reassure him that whether or not he committed the crime, God and I loved him. Eventually, I received a letter back from Dre, and we became penpals.

     In the first letter I received from him, he said I was the first person he thought of when he went to jail. As we continued our correspondence, he opened up to me the way I had always hoped he would. When we were kids, he didn't always say what was on his mind, but now his thoughts and emotions flooded off the paper like a raging river. We wrote well over one hundred letters within a few short months.

     My twenty-fourth birthday was on the horizon. Sadly, the only thing that I can remember the day before my birthday, was my sister and brother-in-law sitting my mother and I down to give us six months to find somewhere else to live. It had been pretty rocky with me being there since I'd arrived. I was given the option to help out more than I already was, or get out. Feeling hurt, I decided to leave the next day.

     I didn't want to be anywhere that I wasn't wanted. I had no where to go, but I asked a friend of mine if I could stay over one night to figure out what I was going to do. That night, my mother texted me to say that she wasn't going to stay at my sister's either, so we moved out the following Sunday. We rented a U-Haul and got all our belongings out of the house within two hours while my sister and her family were at church. We got a storage unit and slept at a hotel for a night, only to then sleep in our broken down 98' Lexus. We were homeless in our own state, something we never thought would happen. For a week, we showered at a gym just like we did in California. My mother's co-worker happened to mention that she was looking for someone to rent her garage. We took a look at it and decided to take the offer.

Soon after that, Nick called to tell me that he was sending me to *Wild'n Out* in Atlanta on October 30th. I was excited to go to Atlanta as I'd never been. I was feeling torn between being grateful and uncertain. I didn't like the thought of leaving my mother alone in a garage, yet I was anxious to get to work to help change our situation. I probably shouldn't have even gone on that trip, as I was in such a terrible state of mind.

Right before I flew to Atlanta, TyRay the manager of Yvng Swag, hit me up to do a collaboration with Swag. Not wanting to step on anyone's toes, I asked The Associate if it was a good idea, and he told me to go for it. After getting approval, I let TyRay know I'd be more than happy to collaborate. TyRay said that Swag and I could probably connect in Atlanta, because he'd be there for *Wild'n Out* as well. I let TyRay know that if there was any free time, we could try to make it happen. If there wasn't time to meet, Swag and I could touch base at a later date.

Once I arrived in Atlanta, I was told to correspond with a lady involved with the camp if I had any concerns. I was driven to a beautiful Airbnb where I made myself at home in the master bedroom complete with a huge bathroom and a gorgeous view.

Not wanting to feel so isolated, I texted a guy I used to know who was going to college in Atlanta. I let him know I was in town and asked if he wanted to stop by and stay with me for the night because I was afraid to be alone. Thankfully, he showed up and we were able to catch up.

I documented everything on social media while I was in Atlanta. I didn't want to feel depressed the whole time I was in town, so I did all I could to keep busy and not be alone. My two week stay was filled with back-to-back studio time, being on the *Wild'n Out* set at Tyler Perry Studios, and filming music videos.

On November 8th, 2018, we filmed the "Simple" music video featuring Hitman Halla as my leading man at Moorehouse College. A young guy named ShowTime Brando let us use his dorm room to conduct the love scene between Hitman Halla and myself. Brando also filmed a lot of behind the scenes for me. Everyone else filming with us was well equipped for the cold weather conditions, while I was sporting a crop top and thin jeans. It was a lot to endure while going through a truck-load of emotions, wondering if all the work I was putting in was going to pay off.

Looking back at all the footage on Instagram and YouTube, I masked my pain pretty well. During my stay, I also made the mistake of confiding in certain people I shouldn't have. I felt like I was being sabotaged. The lady in Nick's camp that I was told to correspond with, told me to keep my head down, go with the flow, and even to suck up to The Associate to get what I wanted. I wasn't raised to be a kiss-ass though.

Since I couldn't trust anyone, I let out my feelings into each song I wrote while recording at Patchwerk Studios. I expressed my pain, depression, heartache, and uncertainty as if giving a play-by-play of my inner thoughts. It seemed like no one really listened to me unless my words were accompanied by a melody. I was vulnerable and felt invisible. I was on autopilot, flying through turbulence and dark clouds to an unknown destination.

I coped by sleeping with the guy I called to come stay with me at the Airbnb. He wanted a real relationship with me, but I just couldn't go there with him. I was beginning to fall back in love with Dre via our letters. I was also still corresponding with the girl from H.Y.P.E, and hadn't yet gotten over her either. I was trying to find some solid ground, but there was way too much going on for my own good.

Nick said they would put my EP out at the top of 2019, and I was hoping to share good news once I was back in Texas. Thinking things were really about to move forward, Nick's engineer told me to pick some dates in January so they could begin preparation for my EP *Overdue* to release. I did exactly what I was told, only to be put on the back burner, once again.

I kept being told reasons as to why all my work was being pushed back. It was hard to believe anything I was told. Instead of continuing to wait, I did interviews promoting the upcoming music videos and EP, hoping my effort would be seen and the gang would live up to what they said. It was like I was in a one-sided relationship.

At one point, Nick's engineer gave me a much needed pep talk. He said three major things I took to heart and will never forget. "You have more at your disposal than anyone in our camp. Find someone who believes in you to manage you. Do all you can while you wait." That was all I needed to hear to be confident in my decision to move on. Once I started making moves, everything began to fall into place for me.

While navigating my career on my own terms, I had some unfinished business to resolve with the girl from H.Y.P.E. She and I had been constantly going back and forth, so in early February, I made an effort to go see her in San Antonio. Somehow I knew that it would be our last encounter, so I made sure to make our goodbye unforgettable. It was a beautiful last moment that we shared, but I was relieved to end that chapter of my life.

While in San Antonio, I also stopped by the jail to see Dre. It was an intense moment for me. When I looked in his eyes, I saw the guy I had initially fell in love with. I knew then that I was letting go of the girl from H.Y.P.E for good, and I allowed myself to fall for Dre all over again.

In mid February of 2019, I hit up TyRay about the collaboration with Yvng Swag he had inquired about a few months prior. I decided that I, myself, was going to find a way to cause a buzz. I let TyRay know I'd fly out to D.C. at the end of March to record with Swag and film a music video.

On March 21st, I touched down in Baltimore to work on the song with Yvng Swag. I had already written a majority of the record except for Swag's verse. Swag booked time at SafeHouse Studios in D.C. I met Tone, the engineer, who I'd end up becoming good friends with. Eight days later, Swag and I filmed the music video for the song "Say My Name."

While I was in town, I also ended up performing with Swag. This performance caught the attention of The Associate, who then invited me to perform with Justina Valentine back home in Dallas on April 11th. Everything was moving at a fast pace, and seemed to be working in my favor.

I was flying back and forth, knocking out shows. On April 13th, I was in Philly at The Pink Sotano, and the next day I was at The Fridge in Washington, D.C. Between shows, I stayed at TyRay's family home. One night after the first show, TyRay sat me down and asked me to tell him my story. I think he was wondering what was going on with Nick's Camp, and why I wasn't being used more or able to make any money.

I told TyRay everything, and he was shocked. I poured my heart out to him. Most people couldn't do anything about my situation, didn't care, or overlooked it entirely. After our first heart-to-heart, we had another, and he eventually offered to manage me. I entertained what he had to say, because I had nothing to lose. TyRay ended up breaking down how the music industry worked. He answered every question I had previously been kept in the dark about.

During all the ups and downs, I constantly prayed to God. I asked him to make it obvious to me who should be guiding me in my journey. Because of TyRay's transparency, I knew he was the one. I don't trust many people, let alone men. However, with TyRay, there were no red flags in comparison to some of my recent experiences.

I went back to Dallas with a fresh mindset and a new manager. I performed with Justina Valentine, then headed straight to Miami to meet up with a journalist who wanted to interview me. She found a place for me to stay, had two shows lined up for me, and we took Miami by storm.

The first day I was in Miami, the Associate called me and asked what I was up to. Nick and The Associate came to Miami and invited me to a club called Story. My friends and I had a full schedule from going to the Wild'n Out bar, photo-shoots, and causing a frenzy on Ocean Drive, so we decided to throw Story in as well.

Once we got to the club, The Associate guided us through the club to Nick's section. Nick was handed the mic and made shout-outs including one to Natalie Nichole. The DJ then cranked up "God's Plan" by Drake. That moment was monumental. Everyone roared as soon as they heard the intro. I vividly remember looking at The Associate and Nick, then at my friends, knowing there was a universal shift about to take place. We recited every word to the song at the top of our lungs, and it was freeing. I was able to leave that club with my head held high knowing I was onto bigger and better things. Once I got back to Texas, I started a new chapter in my life.

After witnessing and observing other artists' experiences, I realized I wasn't the only one that had career complications while around The Associate. However, it appeared that the other artists were more enticed by small perks here and there over moving forward in their career. I decided to branch out and continue working to make my dreams happen. I was designed to leave my destiny in God's hands, not anyone else's.

9
Becoming
The Queen Dove

I was done playing the waiting game and dealing with anxiety and depression. TyRay and I mapped out our plan of execution, and got to work. The first thing on the agenda, was to release a new single. TyRay used "Simple" as an example of what he could do marketing-wise as my manager. I went from twenty-five monthly listeners to forty-thousand monthly listeners. I also went from less than one thousand streams on my record to thirty-thousand streams in just a week and a half! TyRay was the real deal. I knew it even before I saw the numbers. I was ready to meet his marketing abilities with my work ethic and skill.

Initially, I had no beats or producers to work with. Ty sent me beat packs to choose from, so I could begin writing. I liked seven of the tracks, and "Slide" was amongst the babies I was about to give birth to. Something about that beat caught my attention, and it didn't take but five minutes to write the song. I only spent $25 to go to the studio to record it and $50 to mix and master it with my boy Tone. TyRay then signed me up for the distributor United Masters, and we scheduled for "Slide" to release May 15th, 2019.

Four days after it was released, Slide was #64 on the R&B/Soul Charts on iTunes. I can't tell you how amazed I was when I got the news. I cried so hard, finally being able to reap a reward from all my hard work. The game plan was to release a song every month. By June, I released my second single "Go

Off," and it hit the top 200 on the HipHop/Rap Charts on iTunes on June 28th.

I was floored by what we were able to do in just two months. My first check from United Masters off of "Slide" was $114.94. That amount may sound hella small, but when you've worked for over a decade and made little to nothing, it's a big deal.

TyRay called to congratulate me, and we both cried. What made it all the more touching was, he was crying because he was able to help me make my first check, while I was crying because I was able to pay him back. It was a selfless moment, the type you would have with a parent. He was like a father to me in that instant, and I could tell he was proud of his daughter. With this success, I thought how ironic it was that I could have a celebrity involved in my career and get no results, but with TyRay, I was beginning to fly. It's crazy how one unassuming person, equipped with the proper knowledge and strategy, can accomplish great things in a short amount of time.

In August, I released a single titled "Creative." Soon after, I got a call from Nick's bodyguard asking me questions like, "Are you still waiting on Mr. Cannon, or are you going to do it like Kehlani did?" I was curious as to how she did it, so I could take some notes. Haha. It was a brief call, and I shared that I was doing all I could while I waited. I also said that I found a manager that believed in me. I tried to stay in touch for months while under TyRay's management, but I felt even more ignored than before. I wanted to be a part of the team, but I was an under-valued and under-utilized player. Meanwhile, I was on a roll releasing singles.

I met a girl named Eryka through Instagram, around my 25th birthday. She actually found me on TikTok. She ended up following me on IG, and frequently popped in to watch a lot of my lives. Because of her beauty, she caught my eye, but what really got me was her approach. I get hit on all the time, and she didn't hit on me at all. She slid into my DM's with, "You're a badass!"

We corresponded more, and started to express deeper feelings for each other. Our conversations initially consisted of throwing positive vibes and energy back and forth, and giving short, sweet compliments. I moved slow. However, I knew my ultimate goal was to make her mine, despite her living in New Mexico.

Because I liked her so much, I told her the truth about Dre and how he was in jail. She was understanding of the situation, and made it clear that she still wanted to be in my life. I was happy that she decided to give me a chance. I let Dre know I was talking to her as well, and that I really liked her. He was just happy I wasn't interested in any guys.

I was kind of in a love triangle, which was a situation I never thought I'd be in. I like to think of myself as a very traditional kind of woman, made for one person. I thought I'd either be single my whole life, or one day marry Dre. Never in my life did I think I'd be with two people, love them both, and have them both love me.

In the midst of my personal relationships, work remained my main priority. TyRay suggested that I re-release my documentary *Rise and Shine* on Facebook so people could get a glimpse into a part of my story. It was a great way for my fans to connect with me.

Inspired by how TyRay helped me turn around my musical endeavors, I started my own label Indience Music Group. My goal was to re-create for others what TyRay did for me, while involving Ty in the process. It had always been a dream of mine to discover talent, mold it, and allow it to shine. I happened to meet amazing talent that I presented the opportunity to. It didn't end up working out the way I hoped it would. I collaborated with some of the individuals I found, but ultimately, they weren't interested in the footwork it'd take to get their career to the next level. In retrospect, I realize that because I wanted to help others get to the level I had worked years to get to, I ended up putting myself on the back burner.

Although, I would've loved for that vision of mine to come to fruition, it just wasn't the right time. Everyone has their own journey to walk, and no one can speed it up or slow it down if it's not in God's plan. One day I'll pay it forward with other talents who are ready to be a part of Indience Music Group.

As 2020 approached, I was excited about what was on the horizon. I had a single titled "Tell Him" ready to drop on New Year's Day. The music video for "Tell Him" would premiere on Valentine's Day. My EP *2020* was scheduled to release in March, preceding marketing and promotion in New York organized by TyRay.

After "Tell Him" dropped, I flew to D.C. to finish the final touches on my upcoming project with Tone. When I came back, I got sick with the early symptoms of pneumonia. I finally decided to go to the doctor, as my illness progressively got worse. They said I was lucky I came in because it could've become fatal. Being that sick was the scariest thing. After being put on antibiotics and an inhaler, I slowly got better. I feel like my lungs were slightly damaged from the whole ordeal.

On February 14th, the music video for "Tell Him" dropped, and Eryka flew in from New Mexico to surprise me for Valentine's Day. Before the pandemic hit and everything shut down, she showed how thoughtful she was by coordinating her stay to be long enough to make it to one of my last performances. When it was time for her to go back home, we both reluctantly said goodbye, but something in me knew she'd be back sooner than later.

On March 17th, my EP debuted with 436,343 streams on Spotify. I was excited about an upcoming flight to New York to promote it, but then COVID-19 shut everything down. No one really knew what to make of this worldwide pandemic. It seemed like everything paused. The entire month of April, I was trying to figure out every way to maximize this time. The government started sending out stimulus checks, so I invested mine in a home studio and continued to produce, mix, and master virtually along with booking interviews to promote my new EP.

I was determined to let this moment build and not break me. Before the pandemic hit, I had recorded a lot of my records at my homeboy Louie's studio, The Garden Recording. I knew I had a lot of material that we could finish up and release. I was putting out singles all throughout the pandemic, even more after I built my home studio: Studio N27. On May 1st, 2020, I released a single titled "Sunshine."

Later that same month, I drove to New Mexico to help Eryka move to Texas. Even though she moved in with her cousins forty-five minutes away, it was nice to have her in the same state as me.

In one of the many interviews I had during the pandemic, I met a guy named Carl Michel, who had an IG show called *Youth Empowerment Show*. In this show, he interviewed upcoming talent who might inspire youth to strive for their dreams. Little did I know, he also had a workshop for aspiring author's called Write A Legacy, where he mentored people in the process of writing books and becoming bestsellers.

In the past, I had revisited the idea of writing a book about my journey, but didn't know how to go about it. Carl Michel posted about his webinar on how to become a bestselling author, and I jumped at the opportunity. Carl's webinar was everything I needed to make my vision for becoming an author a reality. I started writing daily.

In December, I got back in touch with Nelson from The ESI Network because I'd been inactive in my acting for 2-3 years. I was hungering to jump back in, especially now that I was no longer homeless. He welcomed me back to ESI with open arms. I began the auditioning process in June of 2021 after getting new headshots, updating all my sites, and getting an agent.

As of now, I continue to write to Dre while he fights for his freedom, due to being wrongly convicted of murder. Eryka moved in with me, and I'm in a happy place in my life. Under TyRay's management, I released my 2nd independent album, *Moments,* that debuted at 1.3 million streams the first day it came out. I'm also auditioning for a lot of roles through

The ESI Network. There are many things on the horizon that I'm hopeful for. I can't wait to keep stepping into my purpose with each new venture and lesson that presents itself.

REFLECTIONS

I realized early in life that I'm a vessel. I'm grateful that God uses me and gives purpose to my life. Whatever I learn through my life experiences, I share those things with others in the hopes that I can help them in some way.

Each chapter of my life has brought many lessons. Throughout the years, I've worked towards growth, bettering myself and others, and achieving my goals. I overcame molestation, racism, homelessness, and continue to fight for my right to be treated equally and valued in business and the entertainment industry. What I've cherished most throughout my journey, is that I have learned to navigate so well through what life throws my way. I won't have to repeat the same mistakes. I have learned how to know better, so I can do better.

It's through the most challenging times in our lives that we tend to learn the most. We learn about ourselves. We learn the skills needed to break through cycles, negativity, or just how to live life. Maybe as you've read about the ups and downs of my life, you have paused to think about your own. What has your life taught you? Take a moment to reflect on what important lessons you've learned the hard way.

I'm grateful for everything I'm now able to work on and execute. Currently, I feel free in my creativity. God never ceases to amaze me. With Him, I'm continually mastering overcoming boundaries every day.

Please share what this book has meant to you and any life lessons we could all benefit from. Use this hashtags:

#ItWasGodTheNatalieNicholeStory & #N27KMOB
be sure to tag me on IG @Natalie_Moments.

Thank you so much for reading. I hope you keep flying with me for the next twenty-seven years and beyond.

You know my motto,

Give love, be love, and be loved Doves.

Keep mastering overcoming boundaries,

Natali

www.ingramcontent.com/pod-product-compliance
Lightning Source LLC
Chambersburg PA
CBHW070943080526
44589CB00013B/1620